7 Step Blueprint to Passive Wealth

7 Step Blueprint to Passive Wealth
Property Management Made Simple

Rob Chiang

All Rights Reserved. No portion of this book may be reproduced, stored in a retrieval system, or transmitted in any form or by any means-electronic, mechanical, photocopy, recording, scanning, or other-except for brief quotations in critical reviews or articles without the prior permission of the author.

Published by Game Changer Publishing

Hardcover ISBN: 979-8-9864117-5-0
Paperback ISBN: 979-8-9864117-4-3

50% of all profits from the sales of this book will be donated to the Operation Underground Railroad charity.
https://my.ourrescue.org/general-donate

www.PublishABestSellingBook.com

"Rob is extremely knowledgeable about property management and investing. As a realtor and attorney I find tremendous value in his 7 step passive wealth program."

Jesse Jong
Lawjong.com

"With Rob's passive wealth coaching program and personal service, our family is on track to earn over $1.5m in profits from 4 properties over 3 years!"

Ann C.

Rob has advised me for the past 15 years and he is a master at simplifying the complex. His straight forward, no-nonsense advice is invaluable and has helped me see through the fog to clearly understand my goals so I am able to get the results that I'm looking for. This book promises many high value added lessons.

Jeffrey Chalmers, CPA (Inactive) and real estate investor
https://www.linkedin.com/in/jchalmers

Rob Chiang and his team are at the top of the industry in acquisition strategies, property improvements to increase rental income, and in resale to maximize profits. Having worked with Rob personally, I can tell you it's rare to find a fool proof strategy on real estate investment like the system they have created.

Ben Strock, Founder of Strock Team,
ranked #51 large team in the US as
published in the Wall Street Journal
https://www.strockrealestate.com/

DEDICATION

*Thank you to my loving wife Mindy and
our precious daughter Hope.*

DOWNLOAD YOUR FREE GIFTS

Read This First

Just to say thanks for buying and reading my book, I would like to give you a few free bonus gifts, no strings attached!

To Download Now, Visit:
www.RobChiang.com/Freegifts

7 Step Blueprint to Passive Wealth

Property Management Made Simple

Rob Chiang

www.PublishABestSellingBook.com

Foreword

Rob Chiang has created an essential book for all real estate investors, whether you are already an experienced investor or just getting started, realtors, or contractors.

I am an unusual lawyer. I am "The Real Estate Investor's Lawyer®" and I'm also a real estate investor. I have had the pleasure of working with the author for years. I've also taught real estate investors and potential real estate investors around the country throughout my career, so I have a pretty good idea as to what real estate investors need to know. This book provides crucial information that can help all investors find the right property management company, ask the right questions, and most importantly, know which property management company is not the right company for the investor's deal.

The "7 Step HEROICS Blueprint" provides important details that guide you from the beginning to the end of what you need to succeed, with language that is clear and simple to understand.

If that's not enough, the author provides an online pre-recorded course, a Live Bi-Weekly Group Coaching with Q & A sessions, and a mastermind, which are all great ways to fine-tune what you read in the book and take yourself to the next level. The "do's and don'ts" when you are looking for the right property management company are not obvious.

You don't know what you don't know. When you read this book, it will open your eyes and make you more confident in finding and working with the right property management company.

Jeffrey H. Lerman, Esq.
"The Real Estate Investor's Lawyer®"
https://www.realestateinvestorlaw.com/

Disclaimer

All the information in this book and on www.passivewealthcoaching.com is published in good faith and for general information purposes only. Robert "Rob" Chiang, Robert Chiang Real Estate Services Incorporated, Robert Chiang General Contracting Incorporated, its employees, agents, subagents, officers, partners, and affiliates, are not providing legal, real estate, construction, or financial advice to the reader in any capacity. The author does not make any warranties about the completeness, reliability and accuracy of this information. Any action you take upon the information you find in this book or recommended websites is strictly at your own risk.

The author will not be liable for any losses and/or damages in connection with the use of our book. Real estate law and building codes and practices vary greatly in each municipality. Some information in this book may also become outdated year-over-year as the laws change with each election. Please consult directly with a local lawyer, CPA, contractor and real estate professional for advice regarding your specific situation. The author holds real estate and contractor's licenses in the state of California, USA only. Building practices will also vary from state to state based on climate and building supply availability. Earthquakes may be prevalent in one area and hurricanes in another. There may be snow in one state and hot weather year-round in another. Please consult directly with a local lawyer, CPA, contractor and real estate professional for advice regarding your specific situation.

Before we proceed, let's briefly summarize what fair housing is and why it's important. Fair housing violations can destroy any property management business, so it's critical to follow the regulations exactly and not toe the line.

Visit www.hud.gov for information on fair housing. Always consult a lawyer if you have questions. Local apartment associations are a fantastic resource. Membership is a nominal fee compared to a fair housing fine! Below is an excerpt direct from the www.hud.gov website.

FAIR HOUSING RIGHTS AND OBLIGATIONS

Learn more about the many fair housing laws enforced by FHEO and how those laws can help you. It is illegal to discriminate in the sale or rental of housing, including against individuals seeking a mortgage or housing assistance, or in other housing-related activities. The Fair Housing Act prohibits this discrimination because of race, color, national origin, religion, sex (including gender identity and sexual orientation), familial status, and disability. A variety of other federal civil rights laws, including Title VI of the Civil Rights Act, Section 504 of the Rehabilitation Act, and the Americans with Disabilities Act, prohibit discrimination in housing and community development programs and activities, particularly those that are assisted with HUD funding. These civil rights laws include obligations such as taking reasonable steps to ensure meaningful access to their programs and activities for persons with limited English proficiency (LEP) and taking appropriate steps to ensure effective communication with individuals with disabilities through the provision of appropriate auxiliary aids and services. Various federal fair housing and civil rights laws require HUD and its program participants to affirmatively further the purposes of the Fair Housing Act.

Table of Contents

Preface 1

Introduction 5

Chapter 1 – How Can Property Management Be the Key to Financial Freedom? 9

Chapter 2 – Growing Without Feeling Overwhelmed 21

Chapter 3 – Qualifications- What Do I Need? 43

Chapter 4 – Ecosphere of Owners, Clients, Managers & Vendors 49

Chapter 5 – What Do Owners All Have in Common? 53

Chapter 6 – Maintenance Maintenance Maintenance 57

Chapter 7 – Management Missions (Strategies to Succeed) 75

Chapter 8 – Requiring Tenant Insurance- Why It's So Important 81

Chapter 9 – How to Set the Rental Rate for Your Vacancies 87

Chapter 10 – How to Screen Good Tenants 91

Chapter 11 – 10 Ways to Keep Tenants Happy 95

Chapter 12 – The 20 Most Common Lawsuits to Avoid 101

Chapter 13 – Marketing - How to Get Property Management Clients ... 109

Chapter 14 – Questions to Ask Each New Prospective Client 113

Chapter 15 – How to Set Fee Rates and Scale Up 117

Chapter 16 – Today's Digital World vs. the Old Paper World 121

Chapter 17 – Forms Glossary and Useful Information 135

Chapter 18 – Case Studies 155

Chapter 19 – There Is No Such Thing as a Management-Free-Forever Asset 161

Chapter 20 – When to Say "No" (What to Avoid) 165

Conclusion 177

Epilogue 185

Bonus Section 187

Super Bonus Section 189

Photo Album 191

References 239

Preface

Why should you trust me in the field of property management?

My name is Rob Chiang, and I have been managing apartments since the age of 16. I have 25 years of experience with all facets of investment property, including but not limited to: rent collection, accounting, maintenance, remodeling, leasing, buying, selling and owning. Plenty of mistakes were made along the windy path. This book aims to help others start off in the industry with healthy habits. I will do my best to compress the most important concepts, and practices learned over the course of two and a half decades. This book could take a few hours to read but will prevent years of turmoil from setting off on the wrong path. For example, let's say a yacht leaves Miami with the intention to land in London. If the boat gets knocked off course just a few degrees during 24 days of travel, you could end up freezing in Iceland instead! I hope to create a solid mindset and professional attitude for you to build upon. Allow the lessons in this book to be added to your professional and practical knowledge vault.

I currently control $193M in investment property assets.

This book will discuss how to create, manage and protect generational wealth with very low risk.

Does this book *guarantee* your success? Of course not! However, one way to give yourself the highest possible chance of success is to build a team. The "team" I'm referring to is not the lawyer, CPA, plumber, or secretary; they are part of the operational team. Building a *CORE* internal team consists of a coach, mentor, mastermind circle, positive peer group, and a supportive spouse.

What is a coach? This is not a book about football. The most successful people have coaches, whether it be for life/wellness or business. Coaches help you stay in the game and maximize results. They can help you identify your blind spots early before they become a problem. Coaches also help eliminate doubts and fears that slow down progress. To learn more, visit Passivewealthcoaching.com (you can also book me for podcasts and speaking appearances). There is also a private Facebook group readers can join.

Rob Chiang

Introduction

You need to be familiar with key statistics about rental properties. Let's review a few.

According to www.census.gov, before and After COVID:

"Comparing the most current vacancy rate estimates to the period just prior to the COVID-19 pandemic shows just how tight the housing market has become during the pandemic. The homeowner vacancy rate declined 0.6 percentage points between the fourth quarter of 2019 and the first quarter of 2022, from 1.4% to 0.8%. The rental vacancy rate also declined 0.6 percentage points during the same period, from 6.4% to 5.8%. Taken together, the homeowner and rental vacancy rate estimates for the first quarter of 2022 indicate that housing availability was extremely low by historical standards. It's not clear what happens next. The housing market is adapting to rising mortgage interest rates, and there is still uncertainty about economic conditions and the next phase of the pandemic."

https://www.census.gov/library/stories/2022/05/housing-vacancy-rates-near-historic-lows.html

According to ipropertymanagement.com, "Homeowner vs. renter statistics, reflect a decline in homeownership, with 35% of American households renting their home. The nationwide homeownership rate was 65.4% as of 2022's first fiscal quarter (2022Q1), a 1.53% decline from the previous quarter (2021Q4).

As of 2019, 78.7 million out of 122.9 million households own their homes. 44.2 million households rent their homes. 2.7% of occupied housing units are second homes. 10.6% of all housing units are vacant, up 0.28% from the previous quarter."

https://ipropertymanagement.com/research/renters-vs-homeowners-statistics

According to https://learn.roofstock.com/blog/rental-property-owner-statistics, "About 43.3 million households renting in the U.S. According to Pew/Policy Advice, the total share of the U.S. renting market is nearly 37%, the highest it's been in over 50 years." This means that the demand for rental properties and related services is growing. Either a business is growing or dying. This business is growing.

A popular real estate blog, https://learn.roofstock.com, says, "About 10.6 million people in the U.S. earn income from about 17.7 million rental properties. As the demand for rental housing continues to increase, the number of people earning rental income may likely increase as well." Having these statistics in mind helps you understand how to market properly to these 10 million investors.

More from https://learn.roofstock.com, "SmartMove also reports that landlords own or manage three rental units, with 31% of a landlord's annual income coming from rental properties. Over 90% of average monthly rents collected are $3,000 or below, and 70% of rental properties owned have an average total value $400,000 or less." In other words, getting into the rental property game does not have a high barrier to the entry point. If rental units are too expensive to buy in your hometown, drive to a cheaper area two hours away. Don't go and buy a collector watch or start day trading instead.

Landlords are all filthy rich, evil corporations, right? Well, actually… "Mom-and-pop landlords own about 16.7 million properties with about 22.7 million rental units. Individual investors like these typically own 1 or 2 single-family rental homes or smaller multifamily buildings with 2-4 units instead of large apartment buildings owned by institutional investors," says https://learn.roofstock.com.

Furthermore, "In the United States, between 10 million and 11 million individual investor landlords are managing an average of two units each, many with just one unit," according to a June 11, 2018 article on https://www.huduser.gov. With an estimated U.S. population of 333 million, roughly 3% of the population owns rental property. Count out 100 houses on one block, and three should be landlord occupied.

Just so that one is also aware of the splits between a DIY (Do It Yourself) owner and a delegator, "When it comes to property management, 44% of landlords own but don't manage their property, while 45% are owner-managers and 11% manage a property for someone else. Landlords who self-manage a rental property handle six calls a year from tenants, while 13% say that they change lightbulbs for their tenants." - https://learn.roofstock.com

CHAPTER 1

How Can Property Management Be the Key to Financial Freedom? (The 7 Step Formula)

Here are the seven pillars of the "HEROICS" program:

Home: Build a farm/brand for your new service/business in the industry

Expertise: Obtain all appropriate licensing

Rules: Designate all assignments to the team members with training

Outcomes: Create leaders within the organization

Insulate: Obtain all necessary insurance, and backup plans

Collect: Software and automatic collection systems

Scale: Profit from & Grow the business 2x, 5x, 10x and enjoy financial freedom

HOME:

- Build a brand for your new service/business in the industry.
- Establish a home base and a farm or network of real estate investor service personnel.
- Build the management brand.
- Franchises are available but also not necessary.
- Advertise on all major websites, such as Craigslist.org and Google Ads.
- Send out physical mailers.
- Establish a property management website with search features. The website should be tenant and landlord friendly.
- Affiliate with local businesses to get branding established.
- Install visible, attractive signage on all of the properties under management.
- Cold call all of the local apartment owners and offer a free rent survey in exchange for their email addresses.
- Advertise on Facebook with an offer of something free, either digital or a "free lunch" to the local rental owners.
- Advertise in all of the local trade publications.
- Volunteer to speak at owner meetings.

- Ask around and see if there are any management firms for sale.
- You could even start as an employee of a management firm to get some experience first.
- Pay to speak or advertise at local trade shows.
- Ask realtors and commercial brokers for referral agreements. Many brokers simply want a commission and not management duties. Be sure to reassure them that their commissions will not be poached should the owner want to sell that property in the future.
- Get involved with local events such as farmers' markets, charity fundraisers, and art & wine shows.
- Advertise on the supermarket shopping carts.
- Speak to the head of the five nearest realtors associations. Tell them that you are focusing on property management and want to know what can be done to serve the community of real property owners in their network.
- Establish yourself as an authority by declaring it repeatedly to everyone in their sphere of influence.
- Buy all the books on the market available for property management and absorb the materials as quickly as possible.

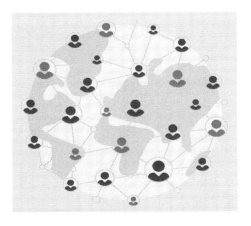

Does it sound like lots of work? It's all about momentum. Momentum comes from using your energy and building upon the little victories. There will be plenty of failures in the prospecting efforts listed above. What's important is to stick with what works and stop spending ad money on those that don't. The great thing about the digital age is the cost per click and customer conversion rate are available to see very quickly!

EXPERTISE:

- Obtain all appropriate licensing. The firm will need a real estate broker's license. According to current laws at the time of publishing, 45 of 50 states require a licensed broker on record.
- Depending on the size of the firm, an in-house CPA and legal counsel can also be valuable.
- If the firm's business plan requires in-house maintenance personnel, a contracting licensee will need to be added to the team.
- Training by local apartment associations that specialize in getting team members ready to succeed in the management field is available for a small fee.

RULES:

- Designate all assignments to the team members with training. Just like obtaining a driver's license when you turn 16. You may be allowed on the road, but you are absolutely not prepared to deal with all the hazards/surprises of the road.
- Team members must be taught their duties and responsibilities and how to cooperate with coworkers. Problems and mistakes are inevitable. It's best to expect some mistakes that come along with the firm's growth.

OUTCOMES (the team):

- Create leaders within the organization.
- Promoting from within is the best policy.
- Team members should be assigned outcomes and rewarded with public praise and other prizes for achieving them.
- The less micromanaging one has to do will help when it comes time to scale. If the business owner is busy being critical of all their employees, there will likely be a high turnover rate.
- The business owner should be working on the business at a macro level. When undisturbed at the macro level, the business owner can make the most important decisions with a clear head.

INSULATE:

- Obtain all necessary insurance and backup plans.
- Form a corporation to protect the business from liability.
- Obtain all required business licenses and insurance policies.
- Errors & Omissions insurance is also highly advisable.
- Business owners should also obtain umbrella insurance.
- Building owners need their insurance coverage limits reviewed.
- Make sure all new tenants obtain renter's insurance.
- Convince existing tenants it's in their best interest to obtain policies (to protect their stuff!).

The management firm should also build a savings account for the inevitable surprises. Even a minor legal case could cost $10K. It's important for the owner to keep as much of the earnings available for the firm to use on a rainy day. If case staffing costs run higher than collected fees in one month during a growth phase, talented staff can be kept on board.

COLLECT:

- Software and automatic collection systems.
- Use AI and robots in the cloud to replace any unnecessary human interaction with the tenants or processes.
- All communication from prospect to active tenancy to move out should be done within a software portal.
- All payments must be made through the portal, which is directly deposited to a chosen bank account. Landlords can choose to accept bank transfers, credit card and cash payments.
- Roommates pay any split they decide on. Cash payments are accepted at a few major retailers using a special barcode.
- Tenants pay service fees ranging from $1.00 (ACH) to $10.00 (Cash). Within approximately three business days, the payments hit the bank accounts. If a payment is going to bounce, it will do so within approximately seven business days.

No more wasted time going to knock on doors and driving to each individual bank. No more chance for human error by the bank teller, the management employee or the tenant who wrote the wrong payee. Guess what else? No more listening to tenant excuses.

SCALE:

- Grow the business 2x, 5x, 10x and enjoy financial freedom. With the properties running mostly automated, a team of 5 people could probably efficiently manage 750 units. If all the processes were still old school, the staffing power of five people could probably only manage 250 units.

- Less staff and more units under control mean more fees collected and less staffing costs. This simple equation equals more profit for the business owner. *The more the processes rely on people, the less repeatable it is.*
- You can acquire a competitor's management business to grow your portfolio. After the transition, the same profit-increasing measures can be put in place. If you or your spouse had a day job in addition to the property management business, you could consider quitting by this Scale & Profit phase. Once enough profits have been accrued, you can use that money as a down payment to acquire an investment property. The passive business now feeds a passive income asset of apartment complexes. Apartment complexes are a passive income asset when professionally managed by someone else!

When most people think of real estate, a real estate agent job with a "sold" sign is probably what comes to mind. Mortgage brokers are probably the second most common image. Insurance agents, escrow, and title officers are also important spokes on the wheel of real estate transactions. Property management is where white and blue-collar industries collide to make magic. For most realtors struggling to broker their first deal of the year, one often dreams of getting into the commercial industry. Property management is a great way to transition into the apartment industry.

Property management is the most recession-proof sub-industry. When the mortgage industry collapsed in 2007 with subprime loans, people still needed a place to live (in apartments). One lesson the pandemic and recession have taught many is that people always need a place to live. A very common demographic is the ratio of roughly 50%-65% renters and 35%-50% homeowners in any given neighborhood. This means that if a city has a population of one million people, up to 650,000 people live in apartments. There will always be demand to manage this industry of renters. This is where apartment management solutions come into play.

Moreover, people need a place where they can live and work from home simultaneously. This home-office-playground-entertaining space called a home, condo, or apartment needs property management. There will always be demand for property management. Robots can't take over this industry for the foreseeable future. Furthermore, during the mandatory COVID-19 lockdowns, the property management industry was considered essential and remained in service. If a tenant called and said, "The ceiling in the dining room is raining," there are no excuses why a plumber can't go there and fix it. Granted, during a pandemic, staffing and scheduling are more problematic. This is in contrast to a hair salon or restaurant that lost 100% of its revenue during the pandemic. If one is a small property management firm with a percentage of tenants who did not pay rent for two years and were protected by the eviction moratorium, then maybe some management was done for free. Most honest tenants who had funds on hand did not take advantage of the system to get free rent.

The importance of screening for great tenants who are well qualified and have adequate savings became apparent during the national eviction moratorium from 2020 to 2022. Typically, no management fees are generated if no rent is collected. If you are a reliable property manager, you can earn reliable income, regardless of the economy or a pandemic. When most businesses were shrinking or vanishing in the pandemic, ours actually grew steadily. Did we still pivot and change our methods? Absolutely! We changed as many virtual processes as possible. However, people do not live on the internet. People live inside physical structures of brick and mortar. Even after a virtual tour, people still want to see their apartment in person before signing a one-year lease. When a tenant reports their toilet is leaking and we send them a YouTube video on how to fix a toilet, they think it's a joke. Therefore, our core in-person service methods did not change.

When person-to-person interactions occur, it is critical for your management team to have a positive sales-forward attitude. Every time a prospect interacts with a leasing agent that could be the beginning of a multi-year relationship. The decision is ultimately emotional when a prospect is shopping for a new apartment. If two apartments have the same features and proximity to work, but one has a rude leasing agent, you can figure out which apartment will remain vacant.

Every time there is an interaction between a tenant and maintenance manager, that is an opportunity to convince the tenant to renew or cancel their lease. For example, if a tenant has a bad leak and the maintenance manager has acknowledged the issue but won't send a plumber after several requests, you better believe that the tenant will find a better or "better-run" place to live. Think of the process you go through in choosing where to eat out. The two most common deciding factors are the food (product) and service. If there is bad food but great service, would you return? If there is great food but bad service, would that be a good place to go out on a hot date? If another establishment has great food *and* service, then the high dinner cost is justified.

In the current environment, people are quite sensitive. It's absolutely essential for the management team to smile, be patient and pleasant with the prospects from first contact to move out and beyond. The best management teams can have the same tenants move out and move back in. Those tenants will also generate referrals from their friends and family. If there are multiple units with related friends and family in the same complex, that's a great sign the complex is well managed. Every position in the management company is a sales job. Let the maintenance team know that "plumber's crack" is not cute, and nobody wants to see that.

Be respectful of time. Utility companies are allowed to give 8-hour time windows because the consumer doesn't have a choice. For maintenance appointments, a 2-hour arrival window is acceptable. For a touring appointment, the leasing agent should arrive 15 to 30 minutes early to test the keys, open the door, open the blinds, pick up the dead spider in the bathtub, turn on the lights, air out the cleaning chemical smell, and check their clothes in the mirror before the prospect arrives (often 10 minutes early!). Everyone has a camera handy at all times. Doorbell cameras will reveal when people arrive and leave.

Every promise the management company makes must be delivered with the correct service and delivery time. Using proper language is also critical to delivering a positive and memorable experience for the owners, tenants, vendors and industry contacts. It takes 30 seconds to tell a vendor or tenant that the team appreciates their time. Of course, the feeling should be genuine. The vendors will remember the compliment and be happy to return for future services. If a tenant is venting about their previous landlord, it is ok to listen, but you should never sit and start gossiping about another business.

CHAPTER 2

Growing Without Feeling Overwhelmed

Have you ever felt like you need help but "can't afford it"? Many operators feel the same way! Whether the portfolio size is 40 units or 400 units, managing both can take eight hours a day. In this book, I'll share the most efficient way to focus your time, energy, and resources. By modeling success, you can achieve greater results ten times faster. Where you leverage (get help) and where you focus your efforts are critical components to long-term success and avoiding burnout.

This book will cover a few key topics within property management that should lead you down the correct path for both "buy and hold" and "portfolio growth" strategies. Once you see the amazing rewards of "smart" labor, there is no looking back.

Let's discuss the difference between "smart" work and "hard" work. Hard work is any sort of manual labor, like digging a ditch for eight hours. A tape measure can measure the amount of work achieved in a day (length x width x height equals the volume of dirt removed by one shovel). "Smart work" would involve renting a backhoe and scooping out the same amount of dirt in one hour. The combination of a "hard" work mindset with "smart" work implementation can make you unstoppable in this industry.

This book is intended to help the owner-operator and any team member managing rental property. The same principles apply if you are an owner-operator or supervise your management team. Do not assume that the property management firm can read the owner's mind. Have a monthly manager-owner strategy call regarding the performance and direction of your apartment complexes. Every question is worth asking so new members can learn. Repeating the same key questions during every business conversation builds the team's memory, so leaders are also formed within the team. Questions such as "What is the vacancy rate?" and "How much rent is in arrears?" are good places to start with weekly update calls.

The best answers require the best questions. One of the best questions to always ask yourself is, "What improvements will increase the value of this property?" The simple answer is *anything that will increase the monthly rent of each apartment.* Conversely, you could continually ask, "What is wrong with this place?" That only generates a long list of capital and/or cosmetic improvements that would make the property perfect in your eyes but also force the property into bankruptcy. You don't need psychic abilities to predict what amenities a renter wants and needs. You can gain insight by visiting neighboring vacant units and making a list of the top five amenities offered.

Perhaps, jokingly, you thought we would talk about the importance of landscaping and our great reveal of the secret plant that drives tenants so crazy they always rent the apartment. Sorry, there is no such secret "catnip" plant for renters. If you discover it, please let me know. We do have a formula that will help you get your properties rented, and we'll discuss it next.

Case Study 1: (2) Bed (1) Bath apartment rents for $3,000 per month. Picture a basic class "B-" apartment in a "B" neighborhood with no A/C, shared laundry on-site and carpeted floors. Here are some straightforward improvements that could raise the market rent for that apartment: Pergo floors (+$25 rent/mo.), wall A/C Unit (+$150 rent/mo.), adding stacked or all-in-one laundry in-unit (+$100 rent/mo.), and fencing off private patio/backyard space if available (+$100 rent/mo.).

With these new amenities, a "Class B-" for $3,000 per month can now be rented as a "Class B+" apartment for $3,375 per month. Now, the unit is collecting an additional $375 per month. That's an additional $4,500 rent per year for this single unit! With an average apartment size of 800 SF, the improvements mentioned above might cost $10,000. In this case, the investment would be paid back in less than 2.5 years.

Increasing the value of your property is great if you are planning to sell or refinance. For example, an 18 GRM (gross rent multiplier) x $4,500 increased annual rent = $81,000 in added value per unit. If you own a 40-unit property, you just added $3,240,000 worth of value while spending $400,000 in capital improvements ($10,000 per unit). You could also spread this expense over five years, spending $80,000 annually.

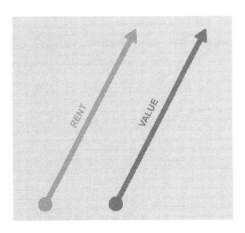

As an owner-operator, you call all the shots and execute. If you hire a property management firm, they will need remodeling instructions and budget constraints. If you're really in a hurry to boost value with limited capital, turn over a handful of units and pro forma the rest. This means you can show proof of concept (remodeling = much higher market rent) and remodel only 15 of the 40 units. Please keep purchase financing in mind when using this strategy. With current cash flow lower than a fully remodeled complex, lenders will require more money down, shrinking the buyer pool slightly.

As a rule, try to keep the remodeling cost per apartment unit at less than $35K (less than 10% of unit value). **NOTE:** This is price adjusted for the Bay Area, CA, where units frequently sell for $400,000 per unit. If one's units are only valued at $50,000 per unit, then please adjust the price of improvements down accordingly to $5,000/$10,000 per unit. Additional boosts to the monthly rent could be converting carports to garages (+$100/mo. additional monthly rent per space) by adding power and motorized doors. Adding individual parking space walls is also an option, though more challenging with the fire code and space limitations for opening the car doors.

Swapping out old appliances with new stainless steel units is an easy way to refresh a dated kitchen. Most delivery services now will even install the new appliances for a small fee. A remodel with good quality materials like solid wood cabinets, and granite countertops should last 20 to 30 years. If you're planning on flipping the property, upgrade the interiors 6 to 24 months before the sale. Buyers like it when the remodeled units have some proven rental history at market rents while the interiors still look fresh.

In the previous section, we talked about improvements that generate a strong return on investment. Here are some examples of construction-related improvements that could cost you a fortune, and renters are usually not willing to pay more for:

- Upgrading three prong grounded wiring/outlets from existing two prong.
- New electrical main/sub panel upgrade, thicker or soundproofing drywall insulation.
- Popcorn ceiling removal.
- Water or wall heater replacement
- Raising ceiling height
- Asphalt or new concrete parking lot surface
- Landscaping appearance and maturity
- Main sewer line replacement
- Putting in a main copper water line.

- Adding a security gate and security cameras, or if there is a security guard.
- Fixing the stucco, siding, and roofing.

These items listed are important and should be monitored for safety issues. However, these items should be placed in the long-term capital expense category, not the added-value category. If you make the improvements that create more cash flow before the expenditures that do not generate revenue, then this relieves pressure on the property operators. Once sufficient cash flow has accumulated as retained earnings, you can then plan for items like a new roof and solar panels, LED lights, etc. Please consult your CPA/tax attorney to see which capital expenditures offer the most tax benefits, such as accelerated depreciation.

After you've made all the improvements you're comfortable with, it's time to rent the place. You should have placed an advertisement and shown the apartment to prospects. The next step is selecting the right applicant from the stampede of renters who want this beautiful unit! Using thorough tenant screening services is critical to the tenant selection process. The more information you have on a prospect, the better. Always go with a thorough tenant screening product. Don't worry about the higher cost. Qualified applicants are willing to pay $30 or $40 application fees, which cover the costs of screening for credit scores, criminal background, identity verification, employment, and more. Unqualified applicants usually don't apply, or their application fees bounce. When this happens, it is apparent they're not the right tenant.

If you hire a property management company, just provide specific and consistent information on the tenant criteria. In addition, always follow fair housing laws. Laws can change yearly and with each new election, so stay abreast of the updates. Laws may be different in each city of the same county. Please consult with a local real estate attorney to get a current legal update.

Repetition is the key to skill. Master violin players spend thousands of hours playing the same chords until they become a master. To truly be a value-added service provider to property owners, you should "master" property management. You may notice that I will repeatedly discuss many of the same concepts and topics because this industry involves many routine processes coupled with a system for dealing with the "daily surprises."

After the prospect is approved, here are a few contact-free tips to make the move-in process as efficient as possible:

1) Sign the lease electronically with "digital" ink, not in-person on paper with "wet" ink. There are many different vendors online who can help facilitate this process. Every person receives a completed copy when fully executed. Other parties that do not need to sign but require a copy are also sent a download link. Cloud-based property management software can also help integrate a word format lease document with keystones that auto-fill the application data into the lease to make lease signing as quick and easy as possible. The lease form will be one-size-fits-all and sufficient for most people. If you decide on this route, it's best if a local attorney drafts a lease form for each property. If the lease is written and signed virtually, imagine how much you'll save in payroll costs! Now, if a lease with more specific details for each tenant is needed, it will still need to be drafted manually or simply coupled with lease addenda.

2) Never lift a finger to collect rent again! Collect rent funds electronically. Waiting for the mail carrier to arrive and then running to the bank takes valuable time away from adding value to other aspects of your business. Tenants can also pay with cash at major grocery stores, pharmacies and convenience stores with walk-in-payment systems. Tenants will receive a unique barcode via email or text, which they bring to any approved cashier. For a $2,000 rent payment, the fees are usually around $12. There may be maximum transaction amounts as well. Please ask the payment processing service for their fees, rules and limits.

3) Install a digital access system. Once you receive the tenant's move-in funds, have the tenant provide their desired door code. Once the door code is programmed, provide the digits to the tenant. No more lost keys or waiting to meet a tenant while they get their flat tire fixed. No time pressure on either party is a huge relief for everyone. Once this tenant moves out, simply change the code for the contractors and again for the new tenant. Just manage the low battery warnings every 9 to 12 months. Some proactive tenants are willing to change the batteries themselves.

Considering the driving time, the contact-free methods listed above could save you three hours of payroll cost per lease.

4) Install a physical lockbox on the doorknob with a set of physical keys inside. A second trip to remove the lockbox will still be needed, but it's still more convenient than the traditional meet-and-greet method. This contact-free setup is also ideal if someone is sick.

Check-in with the tenant to see if they have any questions or concerns after living there for a few days. Here's one of my email templates you can use:

Dear Tenant,

Please let us know how you are adjusting to your new home. This is a friendly reminder that you should have the utilities transferred into your name. Should you notice any maintenance items that require our staff to make a visit, please make a list and send a request through the portal with photos. We will work with you to get the apartment tuned up to your satisfaction. In the meantime, please don't hesitate to contact us with any questions.

Sincerely, Management or (Your Name).

Whether positive or negative, always thank them for any feedback. Now is the chance to prove that they selected the right place for their family to live. Think of each tenant as an impromptu manager. Some tenants are more "vocal" than others, and it is critical to view this in a positive way. It's in the best interest of the owner, tenant, and manager to have the property running properly.

What if a tenant requests a big-ticket item that is not a *need*, but a *want*? Before denying the request, discuss splitting the cost with them. How much in lost rent does one month of vacancy cost the owner? Each tenant will have their own unique design and amenities requirements, so perform all reasonable comfort-related requests.

Some tenants will never call the landlord to fix their apartment. These tenants usually pick the cheapest apartment and assume that the landlord will punish them for sending in work orders—some tenants just believe this. If you have any tenants with this mindset, they need to be retrained.

Tenants who rent a fully remodeled apartment with new appliances will often expect everything in the apartment to be running at 100% at all times and also be cosmetically perfect.

Regarding the exteriors, parking lot and common areas, ensure these areas are exceptionally clean, well-lit, and free from safety hazards. Set up a team of vendors or internal employees to respond as quickly as possible to service calls. The sooner the response, the better the experience the tenant will have. Respond no later than 24 hours for non-emergency work orders. Tenants will treat the management team nicely when their requests are being handled in a reasonable timeframe. If requests are perceived to be ignored, or multiple vendors are unable to fix the issues, the tenant may escalate their frustration into legal threats/action. Be wary of this reality. Repeatedly instruct tenants NOT to text, call or email individual team members because they will get a faster response through the portal. Whether a routine request or an emergency, funnel all work order requests through the portal.

There could be a situation where secondary water/mold damages are occurring. If the employee that the tenant is calling is out of town, doesn't have cell service, and cannot respond, the tenant may assume they are being ignored while the problem worsens! Prospects who turn into tenants often mistakenly assume they should call the leasing agent first. The tenant is contacting the right company but the wrong department. Contacting one leasing agent gives the tenant a 50/50 chance of reaching someone. Contacting the whole team through the portal gives the tenant a 100% chance that the entire management team can see and take appropriate action on the maintenance ticket.

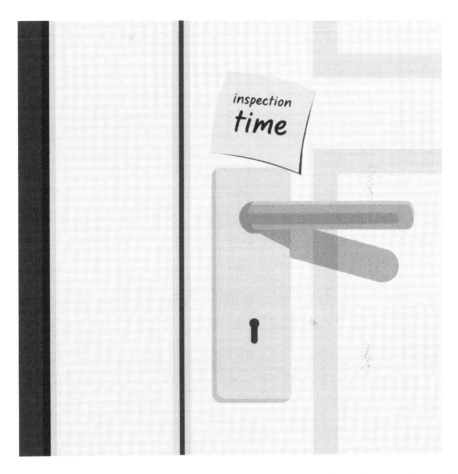

When interior entry is required, send two emails and post physical notices on the tenant's door. If there is a property management firm in place, let them know your expectations in advance. **NOTE** (pandemic related): Assuming everyone is healthy and symptom-free, the best way to formulate the most suitable solutions to the issues is face-to-face. If the tenant/manager desires social distancing, then all parties should be open to sending/receiving photos/videos and using video chat. Obviously, you can't smell over video chat, so pets, smoking, or moldy smells will be difficult to catch unless the tenant offers those clues. There is a high probability that some kind of lease violation is going on inside the apartment if there is a tenant who is frequently refusing entry. Those tenants should be investigated for life and safety issues ASAP. You can call the local fire department to pressure the tenant to comply. I had a tenant who built a whole pergola and outdoor living room and dog run/kennel on their extra large upstairs front patio. This structure posed a fire danger and blocked ingress/egress. After multiple written requests and arguments with management, the tenant still refused to take the unauthorized structure down. With the help of the local fire department safety inspector (free inspection), the tenant finally complied and cleared out all of their belongings within 24 hours. Just like that game *Who Wants to Be a Millionaire?* Just "phone a friend."

Each rental property is its own separate entity. Different buildings owned by the same family or hedge fund are still individually unique. Tenants are the customers. Landlords are housing providers or the "business owners." The customer is *usually* right. The rental market moves in cycles. Some years, it's a landlord's market with short supply. Other years, it's a renter's market with a glut of apartments for rent. In a "tenant rental market," do what you can to please and retain existing customers. Always welcome tenant feedback. Empathize with the Tenant's request, even if their request is being denied. For example, when a long-time tenant requests new windows be installed, but the Landlord is not planning on installing new ones, how should you appropriately respond? Do not promise new windows unless it is already planned. You could say, "New windows are something that is being considered; however, a specific date for this major expense has not been committed to yet. Please check back with us again in the future."

Find out if the single pane windows are a major issue causing interior condensation, mold and health problems. If they are, then replace only that unit's windows immediately! If the tenant just wants windows that open and close smoother and look newer, then the expense can be discussed at a later date. Maybe a better curtains/blinds combination could be an adequate solution for the tenant. Sometimes just talking on the phone with the tenant for a few minutes can make them comfortable enough to renew the lease for another year. After all, moving is a drag!

Please be aware of the activity on each property while staying out of the tenant's personal business. Frequent suspicious activity might require the installation of security cameras, security guards, and video doorbells. Tenants stayed home more during the COVID pandemic. With the combination of thin walls/floors and increased physical fitness activity indoors, noise complaints tripled.

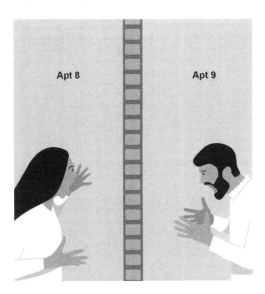

Not surprisingly, a few of the noise complaints escalated into very hostile situations.

Imagine one tenant upstairs jumping up and down during a 45-minute Zumba routine while the tenant downstairs is on a Zoom meeting with 100 of their co-workers. The landlord should believe all of their tenants' messages. However, when a complaint is lodged against a neighboring tenant, proof is required in the form of date and location-stamped videos. 98% of the time, the tenant being accused isn't even aware they were disturbing their neighbors. Once disturbances are documented, and if patterns are obvious, then a specific tenant can be singled out and warned.

Generally speaking, if there is a noise violation at a complex one night, then all tenants are reminded of the noise policy. Most of the noise complaints occur within the walls of the complex. It is very rare for a noise complaint to occur outside, such as a loud car stereo after 10 p.m., because if one neighbor is disturbed, they are probably the only neighbor being disturbed (banging a broomstick on the ceiling). Document any and all complaints between tenants. Encourage tenants to call the police with their noise complaints. If the police can't find anything to justify a report, then there is not much more the property management can do. More often than not, police officers will recommend that the tenants exchange phone numbers and just politely communicate with each other. Tenants can share information voluntarily with themselves.

Landlords must never share tenant information with each other. Tenant information such as race, profession, student/employed status, phone number, email, gender, etc., is 100% private information. If anybody asks (sometimes prospects or neighbors will ask), just respond,

"That information is private and protected information." Do not casually give out clients' information.

Always double-check. Even when there is a written landlord or mortgage lender verification from a tenant who is moving, always double-check with the outgoing tenant that they give permission to release (and what specific information). Do not offer any unnecessary extra editorial commentary to the next landlord regarding the outgoing tenants. If you don't use software for management when communicating official management business, only send out an email blast by using bcc (blind carbon copy)—bcc: everyone. Recipients cannot see all the people the email was sent to.

You've probably been on an email with everyone's email visible when it wasn't appropriate. The sender was probably not tech-savvy. Maybe you've received some sensitive emails intended for another person with a similar name and/or a different last name. Be aware that when sending fresh emails (not replies) from your phone, if one has nicknames attached to the person's email address, please make sure it's professional and applicable. Examples of appropriate tags: "415 Main St Bob Smith" or "63 units Mountain View Bob Smith" for bobsmith1965@anyemail.com would be visible to Bob Smith when he reads the emails. If one accidentally tagged Bob Smith "Bald Spot 63 units Bob," that would be disrespectful and likely end that relationship. Just as when tenants label their spouse "honey ♥ boo boo," it's visible when they send the management team direct emails. Another thing to be aware of includes the "autofill" setting on your computer or phone. It's incredibly easy to type quickly and send emails to the wrong person.

If emails must be written from email software, copy and paste from the software records every time. If there are 35 people with the first name Mary in your inbox, what is the probability that the INcorrect Mary's email address will autofill? What if that email has sensitive information like social security numbers, legal documents and such? Property management software makes it easy to email through software to avoid errors and ensure the message gets to the correct person. For extra added precaution, add password protection to documents. If you need an example, just try emailing your local escrow office and request wiring instructions to understand the process of sending/receiving encrypted emails.

Don't be that unprofessional operator! Don't send a group text to all tenants. If tenants want to share their information when they meet up at the pool, lobby, mail room, gym, or laundry room, that's their choice. As the owner and/or manager, always keep a layer of liability between tenants. It will be extremely uncomfortable to serve a tenant a 3-day notice to clean their carport, raise their rent or collect unpaid rent if they are sitting on your couch drinking a beer! It's best to keep the landlord-tenant relationship strictly professional.

Do you want to see how the building is performing? Order an inspection. Building inspectors are a valuable resource that charges a small fee. Most people only go to the doctor once a year for an annual check-up. Buildings are complicated and wonderful businesses. Sometimes the accounting reports are inspected more than the buildings themselves. Get the buildings an annual check-up because ignorance is *not* bliss! Ask the local fire marshal to inspect your building if annual city inspections are not required. An ounce of preventative maintenance is worth a pound of cure. Spending a small amount of money on preventing a big tragedy will help you sleep better. It might cost $5,000 to fix an aging balcony compared to a collapsed balcony that could cause death and bankruptcy of the ownership group.

Nobody can efficiently manage investment property alone, so get the help you need (get help with your weaknesses, like accounting or roofing). The best strategy is to get out in front of any potential issues. Question the tenants regularly to see if they notice anything wrong, such as malfunctioning timers, lights out, low pool water, potholes, broken sprinklers, dripping water sounds, parking violations, animals and scratching sounds in the attic, etc. Tenants can be shy unless called upon. Some landlords have mistakenly conditioned tenants to remain silent. Some owners think "no news is good news." "No news" is the same as "too quiet." Tenants may think a tub spout that will not stop dripping or a damaged toilet wax ring will heal itself, or a bubble in the ceiling will dry over time, but "no news" will often mean ripping out the entire bathroom after black mold has taken over the bathroom ($15,000). Had the tenant simply reported the leak to management in a timely manner, the fix may have just been a new shower cartridge, wax ring, or overflow gasket (less than $250).

A bad tenant is someone who removes the smoke detectors in their unit so they can smoke various substances and burn the floor coverings. The great tenants are willing to inform the landlord of all perceived issues. For example, a smoke alarm in a nearby unit caught a tenant's attention, who then called the fire department. Even though there was no visible smoke, the tenant still called 911 and the landlord. The tenant in that unit forgot to turn off the oven and everything inside soon caught on fire. Thanks to this great tenant's quick action, they saved the rest of the building and its occupants from serious harm and displacement.

Key points here:

- Always have working smoke/carbon monoxide detectors per the fire code.
- Tenants should be willing to report small issues immediately before they become big.
- One unit incurred minor fire damage instead of the entire complex.

Sending the tenant a $50 gift card is a nice way to say thanks for saving the $5M building from going up in flames. Yes, you have insurance, but who wants to go through the hassle of putting tenants in hotels, waiting for reimbursement, permits and remodeling? A fire repair record also reduces the property's value—a lose-lose equation. The last insurance claim I filed took nine months to pay out. If an owner is tight on funds, that would be a terrible surprise. These types of repairs are usually paid out of pocket by the owner first. Insurance companies send out adjusters. Then they want three bids (complete bids), and it takes time to get approval. By the time they issue a check, the construction work has long been completed. Insurance companies and city jurisdictions usually say if it's a life/safety hazard, just proceed with the work as soon as possible. Hiring a fire remediation company can also cost a small fortune.

Summary: We have covered a few beginner tips on how to create an effective property management plan:

- Get the rents up as quickly as possible and get collections at 100%. This keeps the owners happy.
- Keep the tenants happy, safe and healthy (in regards to the building), and all else will fall in line.
- Keep the tenants renewing their leases, and perform preventative maintenance.
- Repeat 1-3. Now you have an efficient business.

Pop Quiz:

1) Who is your secretary? Answer: _____

2) Who is your handyman? Answer: _____

Answers:

1) Unless you named someone, the person in the mirror.

2) Unless you named someone, the person in the mirror.

CHAPTER 3

Qualifications- What Do I Need?

You should approach the field of property management like golf or chess. The rules are easily learned but take a lifetime to master. The black and white areas are easy to distinguish. For "newbies," the gray areas are the most confusing.

Let's say you are managing a house or two for a friend. Taking this to a professional level requires commitment. Once you decide to be a property manager, you should consider several qualifications. Property management involves a few fields of expertise working in synergy: construction, property management and leasing; you could also throw insurance and financing in there.

What might be your motivation for working in property management? Do you already own a property? Want to work for a company? Want to start a new business? Experienced in some sort of construction?

Let's start by approaching property management from the construction side.

Maybe you are working in construction, busting your back for an hourly wage, and wondering if there is a better way to use your skills to earn passive income. Can you imagine having financial freedom? What if you could get paid a fixed monthly amount to watch over a property, regardless of the number of service calls you received? Would that interest you? Read these next sections to find out how. You already have the skills to do it! It's time to know your worth and earn it!

Construction: Rental property owners are always looking for people with handyman skills. Start as a resident manager or maintenance manager. You can do the job yourself or with your spouse. If you become a resident property manager, you can leverage your wages to include free rent. If you choose to be an off-site maintenance manager, a lot of what you will be doing is overseeing the property. Owners have different requirements for their maintenance managers. Some want you to be hands-on doing all the repairs, and others may just need you to "quarterback" and line up qualified repair vendors. Ultimately your job will include what makes the owner happy while keeping expenses low.

Leasing and Documentation: OK, your handyman skills can get you into property management, but that's just a piece of the puzzle. Maybe you want to get involved in the leasing side. It's wise when you're first starting to outsource the leasing duties or partner with an established local realtor while you're learning. Fair housing laws will dictate how you speak and interact with prospective tenants. Sign up with the local apartment association and start taking property management certification classes.

These are usually affordable and provide basic knowledge and forms to get you going.

The owner is a great resource. Ask the building owner to pay for your certification class! The worst thing they can say is no.

Real Estate Broker's License: Most states require a broker or property management license to manage apartments. Please research local requirements. A business license may also be required. You can get a real estate license through online classes or a local community college. If you can't initially qualify for a broker's license, a salesperson license is a good start. You will need to "hang your license" (work in an existing office) for a couple of years before you can test for your broker's license. Once you get a real estate broker's license, you can start earning sales and leasing commissions. A few sales commission checks could surpass an entire year of handyman wages.

Already Have a RE License: That's a great start. Maybe you're already a realtor on a full commission schedule who wants to supplement your unpredictable income by learning new skills to earn consistent passive income? There were times when I was working as a realtor that didn't get paid a dime, and recurring advertising expenses were through the roof. Realtors are often on a feast or famine income schedule. Management income allows you to supplement unpredictable commission income with predictable management fees.

Repairs and Maintenance: Have you ever fixed a leaky faucet or changed a toilet flapper? Maybe the most maintenance you've done is changing the batteries on the TV Remote! Being able to fix things is a desirable skill and can be learned with time. Initially, you should outsource the work orders to a local contractor, which can quickly become expensive. Doing it yourself saves you and your property's owner money. Sign up with the local community college and start hands-on home repair classes. These are usually affordable and provide you with the basic knowledge and terminology to get going.

General Contractor's License: Building on what we discussed earlier with handyman skills, consider getting a general contractor's license to take it to another level. Learning how to do a job right is important. New clients feel very confident when you can show them you have a GC license. It shows you have invested time in getting the proper training and techniques needed to make quality, long-lasting repairs. *Light Bulb Moment!* The GC license will take some time to obtain, but it's worth it. The GC license will allow you to create additional revenue streams, like subcontracting the remodeling of vacant apartments. If you charge someone $40K to remodel a vacant apartment and your cost is $30K, your profit will be $10K without doing anything except writing the paper contract. The GC license allows you to do that. How many toilets would you have to repair to earn $10K? Quick math tells me that I would have to swap out 117 toilets. At some point, you have to choose: earn money with two hands versus one powerful brain.

CHAPTER 4

Ecosphere of Owners, Clients, Managers & Vendors

When building owners, tenants, managers and vendors work together, the business will run incredibly smoothly. In contrast, when owners, tenants, managers and vendors are at odds, this creates a toxic work environment. Will one eventually encounter a nightmare tenant, owner, or vendor? The odds are yes.

How does a property manager deal with a nightmare tenant? It's very simple, just follow the law and "outlast" them. Just stay the course because it will take time. We live in a time when a tenant who doesn't follow the covenants of the lease and pay the rent is protected.

How does a property manager deal with a nightmare client? The short answer is to cut ties as cleanly and quickly as possible. Recommend and offer a smooth transition to another local management company. The 80/20 rule is true regarding the relationships between owners and property managers. However, the industry norm is more so 20% x 20% (4%) x 20% = 1%. Normally, 1% of owners will be incompatible with the property management company. Incompatibility between an owner and management company can be a problem. If this incompatibility issue occurs once every 100 clients, that should not be a huge concern. However, if it's frequently happening, executives and staff will likely need to engage with professional sales trainers.

Dream clients are like precious diamonds and should feel appreciated for the long-lasting relationships formed through property management. You should send your dream clients holiday gifts, notes of gratitude and respect, etc. It is also important to check in regularly with your clients to find out if anything needs to be discussed.

Management clients are often lifelong clients. Vendors are also often lifetime vendors until the vendor retires or closes the business. Although the average tenant stays only one to five years, tenants can rent a property for 20 years or more. Moving sucks! So don't give the tenants a reason to move. Make their living conditions as comfortable as possible. Tenants should also feel appreciated. Maintenance issues should be fixed in a timely manner. Big maintenance jobs might require more hand-holding and detailed explanations with the tenant.

CHAPTER 5

What Do Owners All Have in Common?

Owners want and deserve a return on their investment. The time it takes to save up for a down payment and buy an investment property could be decades or a lifetime. Some owners only own one rental home. Property managers need to take the job seriously. Many clients do not have a 401k or retirement income streams. The rental real estate *IS* their retirement. Therefore, they expect to receive a monetary draw each month. If the owner receives a funds shortage notice from property management each month, that can be problematic. Assuming no major remodeling or capital improvements are ongoing at the property, the income should cover all expenses and leave some profit (after taxes).

Owners don't want to be bothered with issues that create drama or stress for them. However, it is critical that the owner get brought in before a candle becomes a forest fire. The reason owners get out of the multi-family product is usually not financial but emotional. Respecting the emotional state of the apartment owner is a pillar to building long-term client relationships. Want to create raving clients? Of course you do!

Owners should always have a team of professionals, and property management is one member of the team. The members should include an attorney, CPA, investment partners (if any), lenders, and remodeling contractors (not maintenance). If all those team members are not in place, the client may start asking the property management firm for legal advice or tax advice. Tread very carefully. I suggest always having a list of three attorneys and CPAs that clients can engage with. When it comes time to read the monthly reports or file taxes, the only deliverable item from the property management company should be the reports and bank statements. If the client wants to have long meetings after each monthly report because they do not understand basic accounting principles like debit/credit and prepaid rents, that could be an ongoing issue. Clients need to hire their own CPAs; if needed, the reports can go directly to the CPA first, then the client second. If there are any questions, the CPA can ask the property management firm for clarification, and the issues are resolved quickly. It may never get resolved if it's a comprehension issue with the client. If clients want to manually change their monthly reports so they can "digest it," this should be politely refused. Custom work makes scaling the business very tough, especially when new employees come on board.

Many clients have been self-managing their portfolios for decades. Some often do this on a paper ledger with only two columns: income and expenses. When the reports arrive in their inbox with proper accounting trees, some clients who want to do-it-all and file their own taxes start to panic. The job of the property management firm is to manage the properties. A CPA's job is to analyze the numbers and explain them to their clients. Once roles are clearly defined, everyone gets along much better.

When it comes to legal advice, it's simple—don't offer any. I speak from experience. When it comes to hypothetical situations, always consult with an attorney. Clients can waste months trying to figure out the situation with their tenants directly while delaying the inevitable (most frequently eviction or relocation, etc.).

CHAPTER 6

Maintenance Maintenance Maintenance

Maintenance issues are all urgent—NOW! Landlords' cannot wait for the rain to stop to replace a burnt-out light bulb in the laundry room. A broken toilet can no longer be fixed when someone returns from work at 5 p.m.—it needs to be fixed NOW. Everyone is home these days (during and post-pandemic). We rarely need to make an appointment since everyone is home all day, every day. On the other hand, tenants are more willing to perform maintenance themselves if we provide the materials. Some tenants would prefer to avoid a third party entering their unit unless it is extremely urgent. Smoke detectors via amazon.com have become a common item sent to a tenant's front door. Carbon monoxide detector batteries, pest spray, and heater filters are just a few items tenants are willing to install themselves if we supply them with the essential materials.

Maintenance is an essential business. Everyone needs a place to live. All tenants expect their included amenities to be fully functional. The basic requirements for "livability" include, but are not limited to: Heat/AC, hot water, cold water, power, sewer, flooring, watertight roofing, sealed doors/windows and openings. If one of these critical components fails, a landlord should have the issue resolved or in progress within 24 hours.

Every tenant and vendor should wear a face mask, gloves and use hand sanitizer before entry. Wearing foot booties is also recommended. This process has become quite standardized but is worth mentioning as a reminder. Reminding tenants to have extra PPE (personal protective equipment) for vendors entering the unit is also a good idea. We have also had some tenants request that their unit be "sanitized" at our expense after completing a work order. When is a tenant being reasonable vs. paranoid? Hard to say, but just try and make the best decision for all parties involved.

Ask tenants to keep a distance while the vendor is onsite. When tenants send our management company a work order, they are usually pretty accommodating to the vendors. It is best if the maintenance situation is described to the vendor, and they are given adequate air space to work. We also prefer if the tenant is home to open the door due to the sensitive nature of people nowadays.

Tenants are ultra-sensitive in this pandemic. People are home now more than ever. A 40-unit apartment complex (which previously did not allow business to be conducted) now has 40 work-from-home virtual businesses running in multiple time zones. More cars are home, and more utilities are being used. More garbage piles up. Mountains and mountains of amazon boxes fill the garbage enclosure. It may be necessary to order extra trash pick up during the week just to keep up with the excess. Remind tenants to chip in and break down the boxes.

On the flip side, we have fielded requests to stop cleaning the parking lot because workers were blowing dust into open car and apartment windows. Normally the parking lot would be empty, and windows would be closed because people were away at work in a physical office. Now they are complaining about their vehicles getting dusty because they are home while vendors are doing their cleanup job—it's an unusual situation. What's the best way to deal with this? Sympathize with the tenants and discuss a solution with the tenants and vendors. For example, we started remodeling a vacant apartment during normal business hours, and our tenant next door asked us to stop. Of course, we do not want to interrupt our tenant's important Zoom calls, but we had to find a reasonable compromise. We asked our contractor to work as quickly as possible and continued with the apartment turnover work.

Case Study Example 1: Early in the pandemic, we noticed the water bill double from the previous month at one of our complexes. We immediately took a survey and exterior physical inspection, and there were no reported leaks. We heard a rumor that perhaps the city had made an error reading the meter and would correct the mistake the following month. A couple of weeks later, a tenant contacted us, who stated she had a toilet constantly running. Leaking toilets can be a horrible water waster. She reported the leak but would not let us enter until one month later. She had a terrible fear of COVID-19 due to a senior citizen living in the unit. This put us in a difficult situation. Should we use the keys for entry with proper notice? Will the tenant pay for the utility overuse? Is secondary damage being caused by the leak? After repeated requests to cooperate with us, the tenant finally committed to a firm entry date, and the repairs were completed. Luckily, there was no secondary water damage.

Case Study Example 2) California is burning again for how many years in a row now? Tenants cannot leave the house because of COVID and can't open the windows because of wildfires. Are we now forced to provide A/C as a habitability issue? Well, the apartment didn't come with A/C, so you don't have to provide it. However, it is good to keep tenants happy. There are reasonably priced through-the-wall units that run off 115-volt outlets. Some landlords have even bought portable A/C units that they loan out to tenants on extreme heat days. Some older properties combine multiple rooms on one 15-amp circuit. One solution available to landlords is first to check the subpanel. If the unit is occupied and there is space (empty breaker slots) on the subpanel, run a dedicated circuit directly below the subpanel. The Tenant will then be responsible for running their portable AC to the desired location. In a show of good faith, the Landlord provided a plug they were not required to.

With an occupied unit, it is best not to create any lead-based paint/asbestos dust in the apartment. In other words, if the subpanel is in the back bedroom closet and the tenant wants their portable A/C in the living room, don't agree to cut, patch and paint 40 feet of drywall unless you know all the risks. Try to find a solution to the problem without exposing yourself to legal issues. Furthermore, ensure that the tenant's A/C is set up properly and does not create mold or water damage from the condensation exit. Do not allow window A/C units to hang off 2nd story windows.

What has changed since the pandemic? The procedure to change a garbage disposal has not changed. The tools and parts are the same. The appointments, personal protective equipment and attitudes have changed. With the rental market turning on its head, tenants are now in charge. Landlords should do reasonable upgrades to the apartments while the units are occupied. If a Landlord can get a tenant to renew for one year by installing new appliances in the unit (at a cost less than one month without rent), that is a good decision.

Managers and owners frequently want to maximize their cash flow by having their buildings fully leased with minimal expenses. In turn, does this mean landlords should let the buildings fall into disrepair to keep paper cash flow high? There is a delicate balance between lean-and-mean, neglect, and overbuilding. Maybe someday soon, an artificial intelligence program can decide which repairs to do and which to delay. For now, human employees will need to make these kinds of decisions.

What is an optional repair? Any request that is cosmetic, such as replacing a 20-year-old, fully functional refrigerator with dents in a few panels. Ignoring a "minor" roof leak work order will cause a "major" repair bill in the future. With the price per apartment unit for sale increasing all across the country, this spread becomes increasingly important to track. Make more money by increasing income and decreasing expenses. The difference between a property running at 30% (of gross income) expenses vs. 40% (of gross income) expenses makes a huge difference when it comes down to cash-on-cash return. In the following paragraphs, we will discuss specific examples of how to operate in the gray zone.

The only truly useful information we have to offer in this book are the items on which the reader will actually take action! Hopefully, you are taking notes on action items you can perform today to improve your property, people, or process.

After sending out the owner distributions each month, you fund the maintenance budget. How do you stretch your budget out like the wings of an eagle? The simple answer is to prioritize spending on those items which are the most important and urgent. Keep the rest of the repairs on hold until capital allows. Your priorities should be to address habitability issues rather than liability or comfort issues. When tenants send in work orders that are cheap but non-essential, go ahead and take care of it. Smaller problems are often precursors to larger issues that can escalate into habitability and liability matters. The easiest way to do this is to complete periodic maintenance surveys with the tenants. You can perform a maintenance survey/smoke detector inspection every three to six months. This is not an attempt to increase the expenses! You're showing the tenants that management cares and makes them feel appreciated and that you will take care of those small items before they become larger issues.

Encourage tenants to speak up when they see something happening at the property. This does not mean that the tenant has become a "tattletale." Tenants can better identify some things a management company or an owner might easily miss. Whether it's an issue inside their apartment or in the common area, they should be met with gratitude and appreciation when they speak up. That sprinkler head shooting a stream of water in the air from 3 a.m. to 3:15 a.m. would not be information the landlord would know by inspecting the property at 1 p.m. If vermin are spotted running into the outside crawl space door, pest control can block the entrances and take care of them before they multiply. The turnover rate will decline when tenants appreciate that you respect their need for a functional and healthy space.

Respect works both ways. Help educate tenants to appreciate their own and shared appliances. In complexes with frequent interior appliance service calls, the appliances in the laundry room are frequently misused and damaged by plastic gloves, door hinge abuse, etc. When appliances are out of service (washers, dryers, stoves, etc.), tenants will not be able to wash their clothes or cook dinner for their families.

Fix what is broken in a timely manner to avoid the "broken window theory" (visible signs of disorder and misbehavior in an environment encourage further disorder and misbehavior). If a clogged toilet is a frequent occurrence in the same apartment, search for the root cause of the issue. No pun intended. Are there tree roots that have infiltrated the pipe? Has the tenant placed a foreign object inside (a ball, shampoo cap, dental floss, or sanitary napkin)? Did this occur shortly after they moved in or halfway through their initial term? Did the vendor take a photo of the cause or make notes on the receipt? In good faith, it is good to pay for the first toilet clog. However, when you get two or more calls for the same issue, it's time to do some investigative work. If one can identify that the clog was due to the tenant using some foreign object such as "flushable" wipes or feminine products, this may be the time to tell the tenant that they are responsible for paying for the cost of the repair. When it happens again, make the tenant pay for the 2nd service call. Something that can also work is to offer to split the cost of a new toilet. If the toilet is less than a couple of years old, it is highly unlikely that it is defective. The wax ring may not be installed properly if it's an extra thick floor (layers of vinyl on top of layers of tile). Talk to the tenants and inform them that the faster management has all of the information, the faster they will receive a working toilet again.

Back to the possible issue of tree roots, a periodic sewer camera inspection should be ordered. A sewer camera inspection can accurately detect the length and depth of root intrusions, pipe bends, breaks, or standing water. Many local municipalities now require a property line cleanout and sewer line inspection at the time of sale. For the jurisdictions that do not require them, it is still prudent to order one and pay out-of-pocket. If cabling a drain costs $120, the cost of a camera inspection is usually around $300. Some property owners like to have this done once per year. The dentist x-rays your teeth once a year to catch any issues early, so why not your property's plumbing system as well? Does the property have all the proper drain cleanout locations and proper size piping? Does a toilet need to be pulled out in order to clear the drain (very inconvenient!)? Every modern building should have a 4-inch ABS drain cleanout access at the end of each main line (outside). Because each drain pipe is simply a straw, each building will need its own cleanout.

Another maintenance feature that is awesome to have is an exterior cleanout at each kitchen sink P-trap is also awesome to have. If you can convince your clients to get these installed, do it. If the building is getting steel pipes replaced with copper or PEX pipe, choose the additional cost option for individual unit water shutoffs. This feature is an absolute game-changer when it comes to plumbing issues. Most complexes around 50 units or less do not have this feature. This will avoid turning off the water main or hot water system every time a shower needs to be remodeled or an angle stop valve is replaced.

Each time that the maintenance crew has to turn-off/turn-on the hot water system, it kicks up large chunks of sediment into the pipes. The older the pipes in the building, the more prevalent the problems with sediment. Where does all the sediment go? The minerals, which resemble tiny clumps of sand and iron, end up clogging the faucets, toilet fill valves, shower heads and shower controls.

For example, the issue you might be solving (bad shower cartridge in apartment #2) required a water shut-off. A couple of hours later, the hot water is turned back on. When the water gets turned back on, the sediment that has settled on the bottom of the hot water heater tank gets recirculated through the whole system, shoots through the pipes, and clogs the shower controls in apartment #6.

At times, it can feel like playing that famous arcade game where you whack little critters coming out of the hole (Whac-A-Mole). You "whack" one problem, and another rears its head a second later. The "solution" to one problem causes collateral damage when tenants immediately report two NEW problems.

In the property management business, it's best practice to reward tenants who are transparent. For items that need repair or replacement while the tenant is still occupying the unit, just get it done. Let us say you have a tenant who loves to cook for their family with big heavy pots. Every time you inspect the apartment, they are cooking with a passion. From a maintenance perspective, if you had put the cheapest electric stove you could find in the unit, those pots may cause the coils to be replaced every three to six months. All the grease spilling over onto the stove may also create a fire hazard. One possible solution is to upgrade to a smooth top electric stove for about $125 more than a 4-coil stove. Sure, it is an additional upfront cost, but it will last longer, and some tenants might even consider an upgraded stove to be an enhanced amenity and occupy the unit for longer than they originally planned.

Water utility and maintenance costs can be a huge x-factor on your profit and loss statement. Greenscape is nice but can hardly be considered as important an amenity as central or wall air conditioning. Having the most lush-looking property on the block can symbolize the pride of ownership; however, water-conscious landscape displays can be just as eye-catching as the green grass while reducing recurring expenses.

Some cities even mandate water conservation by limiting sprinkler usage, such as 30 minutes maximum per week of watering. You could switch from a traditional sprinkler system to an amazingly simple drip system by planting a variety of succulents, bark, and wild grass in an eye-catching design. Do you really need 50 trees on the property constantly dropping pine needles and sap on the roof of cars and clogging the gutters and downspouts? How about having six decorative bushes facing the street at the front of the driveway instead? Tree trimming can cost around $500 per tree per year for fast-growing trees. If you have 50 fast-growing trees, that could cost $25,000 per year. That money is much better spent remodeling one apartment interior or replacing 75 windows. How often has a prospect called a property manager and asked them, "How many trees does the property have?" The answer is probably one in a million.

The first questions are always how many bedrooms, bathrooms, rent, square footage, parking, laundry, A/C, move-in specials, etc. Grass and trees are not a topic between tenants and managers. Trees can create additional liability during drought or extreme rain and wind. The landlord would be responsible if limbs or branches fall off the trees and onto tenants' cars. The insurance for the building will increase with every claim made. Even worse, the carrier could choose to drop coverage after paying the claim! Dry tree limbs drenched with heavy rain frequently result in trees splitting and falling over.

Speaking of groundwater, you should also check if the pool at the property has any underground leaks. Ask the resident manager if the pool needs frequent filling. Find a reputable, responsible company that can locate and fix underground pool leaks. Common area and amenities water utility expense should be monitored for spikes in usage.

What is the best way to save water? Transform the look of a building's landscape by surrounding it with 90% concrete and 10% asphalt. After that, put bars on every window (I'm kidding, DO NOT DO THAT!). Consult a landscape architect for advice suitable for the climate and local water usage laws. Your property should still feel inviting yet sustainable. The property's curb appeal should fall somewhere between normal and unforgettably gorgeous. If the property looks too boring when browsing apartment listings online, it may be overlooked by prospects. If your property and landscape features are overbuilt, it may have functional obsolescence and require a crew of passionate artists who "share a vision." If the property requires a 100-page maintenance manual to be followed, that will be a hassle for vendors. In other words, your property should be able to be maintained by any local and licensed vendor (pool, landscapers, etc.) with experience.

Another pro tip is always picking stock, ready-made paint colors that can be easily touched up instead of repainting entire walls. Any respectable painter knows that color matching from an existing stucco wall is not a perfect science. When painters know that they won't be able to get a good match, they will convince the owner or manager to paint the entire wall, section, or building exterior. Paint formulas can also change over time. Paint ages with the sun and a fresh touch-up may not be guaranteed to blend perfectly. Maybe you've seen walls on other buildings with a gray section, and then a slightly different gray painted on several random spots. If you manage long-term ownership properties, immediately convince the owner to choose one single interior and exterior color scheme. There are plenty of stock combinations available to a designer to make your property "pop" with curb appeal.

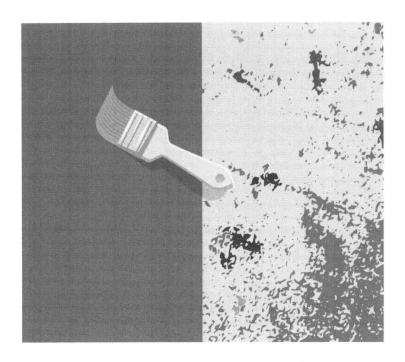

Lower the cost of the master-metered items by installing simple things like LED light bulbs and fixtures, pipe insulation, water-saving shower heads, modern dual-flush toilets, faucet aerators, efficient hot water heaters, recirculation pumps, and eco-recirculation pumps. Ask tenants to help save the environment one eco-toilet flush at a time.

Convincing tenants to stay long-term has great benefits. Besides collecting consistent rent, you avoid remodeling the unit and all the risks that come along with empty units. For example, if you have a tenant who has lived in a unit for six years, and you convince them to stay for another two years, that's building sustainable long-term wealth for the owner. Some tenants are so pleased that they bring in their friends, family and co-workers to rent the vacant units!

Currently, after COVID-19, the key to higher cash flow is retention by all means of negotiation. If one-month-free incentives need to be offered to sign a 12 to 24-month renewal term, strongly consider agreeing to them. Start with the incentives by offering a free blender or $25 gift card and work up as needed. These recommendations assume that the tenant pays the rent on time and is within 30% of market rent. These tenants should also be relatively trouble-free.

This topic is about being prepared for the cycles of the rental market and having the correct mindset. If you take massive action to maximize potential rent collection and reduce wasteful expenses, you can then build up reserves for the inevitable roof, burst sewer pipe and parking lot repair, etc. You will also have money left for the next month's surprise expense: bed bug infestation or a car that crashes into the building.

When you react to maintenance tickets slowly, it inevitably leads to secondary damages and liability. If a tenant reports a pothole after a big rainstorm, that should get filled in ASAP. Throw a $9 bag of Cold Patch Asphalt Repair in the hole until a professional asphalt vendor can look at it.

A trip or fall lawsuit may be commonplace at a shopping center. However, a trip or fall claim at an apartment complex you own or manage can be a real headache. Consider this:

- professionally patch one pothole for $250.

Vs.

- Let one of the tenants or guests get injured, file a claim, pay your insurance deductible, deal with higher insurance payments forever, and possibly policy cancellation.

You will still have to fix the pothole, so you might as well do it yesterday!

For all those owners with older buildings: are the stair rails and guardrails too low and spaced out more than a 4-inch sphere can fit? These guidelines were established to prevent a fall and a child's head getting stuck in the spacing. The code changed, but many of the old buildings did not get retrofitted. As a practical matter and liability matter, get these fixed ASAP. Call a trusted contractor for a permanent solution. To retrofit an existing metal railing system, you can weld new material to the existing metal frame, raise the rail to code, and wrap the pickets with a one-inch metal mesh. Repainting will also be needed after the welding is done.

If the material is wood-based, it's easy to add wood and additional pickets one by one. 8-foot redwood lattice screens can be trimmed and easily tacked on to comply with the 4-inch sphere (child's head) rule.

Another situation requiring immediate response is a reported bed bug sighting. You might be tempted to go to the local hardware store and buy $15 foggers, drop them off at the unit's doorstep and think it's done. Don't believe it! Do not let bed bugs infest the apartment to the point where there are visible dots in the corners of the ceiling and baseboard. When tenants start to show photos of bug bites on their skin, hurry up and act fast!

How do bed bugs end up inside the apartment? Usually, they transfer from used furniture, luggage, "free" mattresses, or couches left on the side of the road. Bed bugs need hosts with a blood supply to survive. Treating one unit for $1,400 now is better than treating the three adjoining units for an additional $4,200! The same dogs that patrol the airports are the same dogs that inspect for bed bug clearance. Once the German Shepherd brings his special nose to sniff around and doesn't find any, the residents can use the apartment like normal again.

Good tenants will keep your property clean and free of pests. Tenants with ulterior motives may let the apartment become infested with pests and stop paying the rent, claiming "livability" issues. Unhappy tenants do not care if the property is in disrepair. If there is one broken window, that might invite graffiti. Graffiti might invite homeless or gang activity. Cars might start getting broken into. The complex might soon be empty. Someone could break into a vacant unit and start a fire—bye, bye investment. One good decision leads to another. One bad decision after another leads to disaster.

Find out if any of the tenants are handy people. If they see something broken in the apartment and want to get reimbursed for the materials, go for it. On the other hand, if someone is trading the non-payment of rent for some construction services, be very, very careful. That is how you end up on those TV court shows. Tenants should be tenants. Vendors should be vendors. It is possible for family members or a vendor to eventually end up in one of your managed units. However, remember not to trade rent for services. Tenants should always pay rent, and vendors should always be paid separately for services.

CHAPTER 7

Management Missions (Strategies to Succeed): Hold, No Remodel vs. Flip for Profit vs. Hold and Remodel

Lowering recurring expenses make buildings worth exponentially more money. That is the value of cost-efficient property management.

When purchasing an apartment building, buyers look for at least three consecutive years of increasing net operating income (NOI). Apartments are a great hedge against inflation and the cost of living. In towns with rent control, rent cap calculators (usually CPI plus a fixed amount of 3-5%) are available online. On the other hand, if the income decreases for three years straight, something is wrong with the building or the operator. Just like a houseplant, either the economy is growing, or it's dying (shrinking). For the U.S. to remain competitive with other countries, inflation should be kept in check while the Gross Domestic Product should keep growing. Buyers look for creative opportunities to simultaneously cut expenses and increase income when analyzing offering memorandums.

Beware of pro forma numbers versus current numbers. It's like dating someone based on what they promise they will look like in two years (pro forma: 50 lbs. lighter, more athletic, and a full head of hair). Always analyze the property based on what it is in reality, TODAY. Ask for copies of the asset's tax returns to see if they match the income statement. There may be significant differences. Are the owners treating the property as a cash cow? Does the property function like a tax shelter where the owners incur as many line items as possible like mobile phone, mileage, auto maintenance, business meals and travel expenses?

Alternatively, if the last two years have an industry-low level of expenses at 30% of gross income, are they repeatable? Does the property have solar panels and individual meters for all utilities? Verify all claims of low expenses beforehand. Be careful when analyzing owner-managed cash flow statements. Often, the owner probably does not pay themselves for their management activities. Just to be safe, look at properties like most lenders do and just estimate total annual expenses at 40 to 50% of gross income. Also, remember to account for the 10% vacancy factor with turnovers.

Purchasing an apartment building involves buying the bricks, mortar, land and the business. This is a simple concept, so remember it forever: *well-run businesses are worth more than poorly run businesses.* The value is related to the risk involved. Fully stabilized, fully occupied, fully renovated apartment complexes sell for top dollar. At the same time, value-add (ugly and old properties) with high vacancy rates and low rents sell for much less. The "golden trifecta" to add exponential value is a lower cap rate + proven higher income + lower expenses.

Is the apartment complex stabilized? This is not the section where structural engineers get excited. This is not referencing earthquake retrofit work. A property that is 50% vacant with deferred maintenance can be considered unstable. If the market rent is $2,000 and all units are rented between $1,700 and $2,000 per month, that property should be considered stable. If the property does not have remodeled units, it can also be considered a value-add. Remodeled units may bring rents of $3,000 per month. It is possible to be optimistic and realistic at the same time. Buildings that are fully occupied can be managed for years, then remodeled when vacancies arise. The front facade can be improved once the higher rents have been established in 20% of the units.

Management companies should touch base with the owners frequently regarding the operations and physical condition of the property. Even with the best local management companies in place, monthly or quarterly input from the owner can correct wrong assumptions.

The following sentence is not an oxymoron. *Budget for long-term capital expenses while maximizing cash flow today.* Owners want their monthly draws on time and hate being surprised by big-ticket items like a new roof. Owners devalue the property they own when they are mentally absent from the management. Owners should be able to anticipate any possible buyer objections in advance of any sales transaction or lender inspection.

Just imagine being an absent-minded or absentee owner that just accepted an offer to sell their property for $10M. During the due diligence period, the buyer discovers $750,000 of deferred maintenance. A proactive owner could have spent $200,000 in all the right places instead. A reactive owner will probably end up agreeing to $500,000 in credits at closing escrow. Properly fixing any obvious building defects without any time pressure and with the best vendor is a recipe for success. The purpose of having property management is for the owners to have free time to spend making high-dollar decisions. If owners want the property management to make the property "as cosmetically perfect as possible with no budget constraints," that needs to be communicated properly in writing.

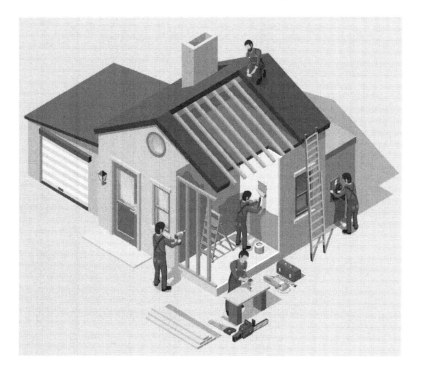

A great example of adding value would be installing a $40,000 solar panel system to save $500 per month and $6,000 in utility costs per year. At a 4% cap rate, that is $150,000 in increased value and $110,000 more than the cost of the solar panels. Any owners out there fixing leaky toilets themselves usually don't have the time or energy to implement innovative value-add strategies. The old saying goes, "Spend money to make money." In other words, be penny foolish and million-dollar smart.

Property management companies should have connections with vendors to get cheaper work-per-ticket rates. It's called the "corporate rate." Ask around to see who is willing to agree to this. Every item that decreases the expenses increases the net operating income and increases property value. At the end of the year, everything adds up or subtracts less!

Which rehab items give the best "bang for the buck"?

- New Flooring
- New Paint
- New Appliances
- Glazing the Bathtub or Shower vs. New Tile
- New Heater
- Adding Air Conditioning
- Adding In-Unit Laundry
- New Windows
- Changing Tactile Items: Locksets, Doorknobs, Trim
- New Vanity and New Faucets

The suggestions above are geared towards recouping the rehab investment in a short amount of time.

For Example, if a $10,000 remodel will increase the rent from $2,500 to $3,000, this is a $500 monthly increase ($500 x 12 = $6,000 annual rent increase).

Ideal time to recover the investment: 20 months + 2 to 4 months remodeling & vacancy = 24 months.

For Buy & Hold investors: Ideal time for rehab cost recovery is between 1 and 3 years.

Here are some quick talking points. See if you can follow along:

- Calculate the property's cap rate quickly!
- Formula: Income minus expenses / cap rate = value.
- Assume properties are trading at a 4% cap rate.
- Example of how banks are underwriting deals now.
- Income - 5% Vacancy factor x 35% expenses = NOI.
- $200,000 Net Operating Income minus $10,000 vacancy factor minus $70,000 expenses.
- NOI= $120,000 divided by 4% cap rate = $3,000,000 Valuation.
- Bank will probably lend the buyer $1.4M to $1.5M in loan. The buyer will need a 50-60% Down Payment.

How to increase the property value- increase NOI?

- Decreasing total expenses is one way.
- Increasing total gross income is the easiest way.
- New Owners always underwrite their own expenses and don't trust marketing packages.
- Pro forma vs. actual. Pro forma is nice to know. Actual is more important.

CHAPTER 8

Requiring Tenant Insurance- Why It's So Important

Requiring tenants to purchase their own insurance policy is the only real way to protect their possessions. For you, the landlord or manager, renters insurance is an extra layer of protection in this litigious world.

For a tenant, it's relatively inexpensive, often less than $20 per month, and shouldn't be an issue except to the most financially strapped of tenants. Pet coverage should also be added to the policy if pets are in the apartment. Most people can add it as a discounted rider to their existing auto insurance policy (if they have one).

<u>Please consult with your attorney on this topic: Why is renters insurance so important?</u>

1. It Mitigates the Threat of a Lawsuit:

The #1 benefit of requiring tenants to purchase renters insurance involves keeping you out of court.

When damage occurs to a renter's belongings, and if the tenant does not have rental insurance, there's a high probability the tenant will try to claim some type of landlord responsibility.

A tenant throws a party, and a guest is injured. The tenant has no renters insurance, and the injured individual has no or inadequate health insurance.

The injured person – or the hospital – files a claim against the landlord. Even if the landlord's insurance company agrees to pay, substantially higher premiums will follow.

A tenant with renters insurance removes the landlord from the picture and from liability.

2. It Reduces Landlord (LL) Responsibility:

If the worst happens and there's a fire or other disaster, you might feel responsible for finding the tenants a temporary place to stay.

In certain states, you are considered responsible and must provide relocation benefits. To make things worse, while dealing with the property damage, LL is also trying to negotiate lodging or other necessities on the tenant's behalf.

Tenants with renters insurance don't have to rely on the Landlord's goodwill or ability to pay for their temporary housing. That's their insurance company's role. The LL shouldn't have that hassle while trying to get a handle on their own losses.

3. It Weeds Out Bad Tenants:

If the Landlord requires renters insurance and the applicant complains that they can't afford it, that's a red flag. If someone can't afford to pay the low monthly renter's insurance rates, how close to the edge are they living? What are the odds that they won't have the monthly rent money?

4. It Covers the Deductible:

If a tenant damages the building, such as inadvertently causing a fire, the LL's insurance policy may pay the repair costs. However, the LL is still stuck paying the deductible, which can be a substantial amount of money.

If the tenant *does* have renters insurance, the policy should cover the homeowner's insurance deductible; making an unfortunate situation somewhat easier to deal with.

5. It Gives both Landlord and Tenant Peace of Mind

It's hard to put a price on peace of mind, but knowing the tenants have renter's insurance helps fund it.

Realizing the Landlord won't face lawsuits and pay the accompanying legal fees for issues that aren't the LL's responsibility takes the pressure off. Dealing with a tenant's personal property damage or loss is not fun.

It should also improve your relationship with all the insured tenants because the LL is not viewing them as prospective litigants should they experience personal emergencies.

6. Perform Annual Checks

Just because the tenant showed the LL proof of rental insurance when signing the lease doesn't mean he didn't let the policy lapse. The software should send an alert when the policy expires.

For best results and continued peace of mind, have the tenant show proof of insurance annually as a requirement for renewal. If renters insurance is a mandated part of the lease, the tenant's canceling or allowing the policy to lapse is grounds for termination.

Why are interior inspections every six months crucial (building health check)?

- Reveals unreported issues.
- Reveals overcrowding, such as two beds in the living room.
- Unreported maintenance like leaks or mold.
- Document everything worth noting with photos, dates and unit #s.
- Don't take photos of anything personal due to privacy rules.

- Gives tenants proper notice and the chance to be present since interviewing a tenant on the spot onsite is the best way to get all of the information.
- Ask tenants to report any known issues going forward.

Have a couple of handymen and routine materials onsite during the inspection (smoke detectors, faucets, etc.). Simple fixes can get done ASAP without re-serving notice to enter and hoping things work out.

Schedule the inspection for all day so the handyman can have access without having to schedule a second day of entries. Sometimes tenants have someone sleeping or a baby crying and want the landlord to "come back later."

CHAPTER 9

How to Set the Rental Rate for Your Vacancies

Always aim for at least 1% of the per unit price or higher. If a unit costs $200,000, the monthly rent should be $2,000 or more. If it's any less, the cash flow could run negative. This metric is based on a new purchase analysis. Over time, rents increase 5% to 9% annually, and long-term investors benefit.

    Here are some points and questions to answer prior to releasing the vacant unit to the rental market. Overestimating the rent value/month unique qualities of the property versus normal market apartment can cause delays in occupancy. Get an outsiders opinion. Knowing the *actual* class and location grade of your unit is critical. Is it a class A, B, or C Apartment? Is the location an A, B, or C? Over-upgrading over the neighborhood doesn't make financial sense. Is the property A condition in a C neighborhood? Do not expect the best returns for that imbalance. B location and B condition can be the best properties to cash flow. Know the neighbors and what they are charging for rents. Study the comps and start $100 less than the competition. Renting fast in two weeks is better than renting in three months for slightly higher rent.

$2,500 contract rent x 12 months= $30,000 annual rent.

$2,700 contract rent x 11 months= $28,600 annual rent.

Rent seems too low now? First, get the tenant in and then raise the rent next year.

Is the goal to sell it or rent and hold? There are various strategies for both motivations. Rental rate is more important to tenants than low deposit, free microwave, promotions, utilities included, etc. Is it summer hot rental season or slow winter season? What if there are no good applications after 30 days? It's time to lower the rent.

Lower rent = more applicants = choose the best application.

Some landlords prefer to rent units for cheaper amounts so they can choose the best application from a large group of applicants. The higher the asking price, the smaller the renter pool who can afford it.

$$\$2,500 \times 12 \text{ months} = \$30,000 \text{ annual rent}$$

$$\$2,700 \times 11 \text{ months} = \$28,600 \text{ annual rent}$$

Additional streams of rental revenue:

- Laundry Income
- Vending Income
- Storage Space
- Parking Space
- Rental Furniture - "Furnished"
- Pet Rent
- Telecom and Media Deals, WiFi
- Utility Reimbursements

CHAPTER 10

How to Screen Good Tenants

Attractive advertising and professionalism attract the most qualified prospects. Conversely, an ad with a blurry, upside-down photo and a leasing agent that doesn't pick up the phone will likely attract a more desperate tenant.

The importance of selecting the right tenants became paramount during the pandemic and the eviction moratorium that was put in place. Many tenants kept paying their rent. Others stopped because they lost jobs and didn't have money, while others stopped paying because they didn't have to; some didn't pay for more than a year. This just hammered home how critical it is to select the most qualified applicants.

Most importantly, government subsidized tenants (Section 8) never stopped paying the rent during the pandemic.

Key Elements to advertising:

- Floor Plan
- Professional Photos
- Drone Shots
- Staged model apartment

- Inviting marketing materials
- 3D Matterport for great virtual tours

Crafting an excellent ad:

- Use exciting language
- Always Include Pictures
- Do Create an Interesting Headline (Examples)
    - *$1500/1BR Beautiful Units with Great Amenities*
    - *$1500/1BR Gorgeous Units in a Luxury Building. Washer/Dryer in Units*

- *Charming 2 BR on Lovely Tree Lined Street - Renovated 1 BR with Utilities included*
  - *Must See! Updated Kitchen and Parking Included!*
  - *Spacious Condo. 5 Minute Walk to the Metro*
- Make It Easy to Read
- Tell the Truth, acknowledge the property's faults first, then sell the good qualities
- Follow Fair Housing Laws

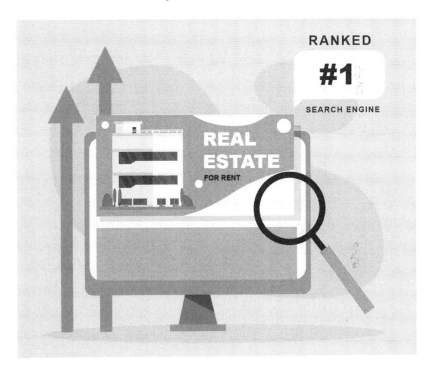

Where to advertise:

- Zillow
- Facebook
- Hotpads
- Trulia

- Redfin
- Craigslist
- Apartments.com
- Rentcafe
- Physical signage
- Local paper, depending on area demographics, can be in other languages

Tips for successful open house & appointments:

- Pre-Screen the tenants on the phone
- Be Excited
- Sound Excited, look forward to seeing them in person
- Good lighting
- Nice smells
- Leasing agent should wear presentable clothes
- Have application & Rental criteria ready
- Make the process smooth

Pop Quiz: (Yes or No)

1. Have you ever regretted approving an application to rent?
2. Do you always run a credit check on all your applicants?
3. Do you run a criminal background on your applicants?

If you answered yes to question number one, you probably answered no to at least one of questions 2 or 3. You should ALWAYS order a credit report and full background check on ALL prospective tenants. If you don't, you better have an eviction attorney on speed dial!

CHAPTER 11

10 Ways to Keep Tenants Happy

Getting tenants can sometimes be hard enough, but keeping them, especially in today's volatile economy, is the real key to building consistent, reliable income. Let me give you a place to start.

10 practical things that will help you keep your tenants happy:

1. *Fix maintenance items fast & always sympathize with their requests.* Tenants need their work orders handled properly and promptly. More importantly, they should feel like all of their needs are being met and never ignored. Even if the request to upgrade or remodel the apartment seems ridiculous, just understand the reasons behind their request. Genuinely propose the request to the owner and relay the message back to the tenant whether it's a yes, no, or maybe later.

2. *Approach tenants for early renewal; they may be shopping around.* Lease expirations should be marked in the property management software at least three months prior. The tenant should be offered renewal at the same rate or slightly less than the top-of-market rate. This will give some incentive for the tenant to stay longer. A

vacancy is worse than a tenant paying 5% less than the top-of-market rate.

1. *Upgrade items that are worn out while the tenant still occupies the unit.* Tenants love to get a new stove or refrigerator—they feel cared for. On the flip side, if the stove is 20 years old and the landlord refuses to replace it, that could be the tipping point for a tenant moving out.

2. *Educate tenants about what the market is doing to rents.* If rents are $400 higher than what they are paying now, then a $100 increase doesn't seem like much. If the tenant is not educated on the comparable rents in the area, they may see the $100 increase as absolutely ridiculous. If they understand that they are getting a $300 break, they might be extremely grateful instead of angry.

3. *Be clear with communication.* Tenants who email more than two times in the same email thread with the same question should be then directed to a phone call appointment. You want to ensure that there is no issue with a language barrier and that all the management communication is understood. Is there a translator in the house who should be the main point of contact going forward? Is there a translator in the management office (rarer) who could be designated for that unit? Is there a pattern of tenants who don't get notices, who always pay rent late, etc.? Improving undesirable patterns should be a priority.

4. *Be available in person.* Some tenants need to see someone face to face. If an issue can't be resolved by email, text, phone, or video call, then that tenant should be set up with a team member to meet in person. Sometimes the tenant just needs to know that they are important (they are!).

5. *Offer current and prospective tenants referral bonuses to build a community.* When existing tenants introduce new tenants into a community, it starts to feel like one big family. If there are cousins, aunts and uncles living in one apartment complex, the odds of any of them moving out are extremely low!

6. *Treat each existing tenant like a new prospect.* Once a tenant moves out, they are not cast aside. They should be treated as if they just showed up to see the vacant unit. Tenants are not trapped once they sign the lease. *"HA HA, sold you now you are trapped, and I won't fix anything!"* Baloney! Tenants should always be happy with the service that is provided. The housing

provided should be safe, healthy, and enjoyable for all tenants and guests.

7. *Provide designated parking spots and enforce parking rules.* How frustrating is it to come home from work and have your parking space occupied by someone? It's 6 p.m., and you're supposed to meet your spouse at home at 6:05. There are no other spots, and it just makes you so angry!! You park on the street way down the block and end up being late for your dinner date with your spouse. Not Fair! The management is notified, and they do nothing. Even worse, if there is one offender, it can have a domino effect with everyone just parking in any open spot. By the end of the night, 50% of the tenants are parking in the wrong spot, and you have a lot of angry people. No emails and no cars are towed. That is an easy way to get tenants to move out quickly. When parking assignments are clear and enforced, tenants follow the rules. Guests do not magically "forget" about parking in open spaces. Once a couple of cars get towed, the word spreads like wildfire. Amazingly, people stop parking in the wrong spots.

8. *Make sure the property is well-lit and is a safe environment.* The property should always be inviting and free of dark corners. People of all ages should be able to walk on the property without fear of tripping or getting cut on damaged wall surfaces or other hazards. The property should be free of garbage, debris, dumped furniture, etc. There should be no raw sewer leaks, toxic chemicals, or offensive smells at the complex. Are there low-hanging tree branches that could knock people in the head? Anything that an insurance agent's inspection would have a problem with should be rectified as soon as possible.

Bonus Tips for Keeping Tenants Happy:

- Before a tenant moves in, walk through the apartment. It is much easier to send in the construction crew when the unit is vacant. Worrying about making an appointment with the tenant and getting their sofa dusty is more troublesome than going in and out when it's vacant.

- Have a final phone conversation with the tenant to recap what type of housing amenities are to be delivered and what they were promised. For example, if the tenant wrongly assumed the property had central A/C before they drove three states to move in, that could be a big problem.

CHAPTER 12

The 20 Most Common Lawsuits to Avoid

I've given you some tips to keep your tenants happy, but let's take it a step further because sometimes situations can escalate, and you could find yourself in court. You never want it to get that far.

How to avoid the 20 most common lawsuits.

1. *Habitability (Is the property livable?)* Could a mediator debate the condition of the property? Is there any doubt that the property is not livable? Does the property have heat/water/functional windows, etc.? Is the tenant damaging the property to make their case stronger? Where did the pests come from? Has the landlord sent professional vendors? Have the vendors been refused entry by tenants? Did the pest control company write up any reports? Did the pest company write up any reason for open food and water bowls attracting rodents? These questions assume the landlord is not a slumlord and is actually attentive and honest. The courts favor the tenant, so the landlord should have overwhelming proof that they are an honest and ethical property owner or manager. Always be ready to prove this to the court!

2. *Using generic or outdated legal documents.* Location, location, location is what everyone says in real estate. When it comes to the contract side: disclose, disclose, disclose. If your contracts are outdated, do this right now: dispose, dispose, dispose. Laws change so frequently and significantly that an outdated lease will not save the landlord money. An outdated lease will cost the landlord money in the long run. All tenants and properties are NOT the same. That's like saying that all shoe sizes fit you the same. Remember the last time you tried on shoes that were one size too small? They felt terrible, right? It's the same with legal contracts. If a contract is written about a complex with parking, storage, a pool and a gym, and this complex has none of those amenities, that would be quite confusing!

3. *Asking the wrong questions during screening.* Please refer to the HUD.gov website for all the current fair housing guidelines. It is critical not to be casual, sarcastic, or too personal with the questions asked to prospective tenants. Always assume that the prospective tenants will take things the wrong way. The leasing team members need proper training before meeting the public.

4. *Setting policies that discriminate against familial status, race, color, gender, or religious affiliation (fair housing violation).* It is one thing for an untrained employee to make a mistake. Having a misguided owner or manager set policies that clearly violate fair housing laws is an entirely different issue. Please be educated on current laws and ensure the office policies comply. If needed, consult with an attorney regularly to review policies.

5. *Making promises that are not delivered.* If air conditioning was promised to be installed within two weeks after moving in and was not, that could be a problem. If the tenant was promised they could have a huge storage space and did not get assigned one, that could be a big problem. If the pool is still green with frogs and unswimmable three months after moving in, that could be considered a decrease in services provided. Just do what is promised, and there won't be any huge problems.

6. *Charging excessive late fees.* It is important to follow your local jurisdiction's guidelines. Practically, 10% is usually the max late fee. The lowest that we have seen is around $35 per occurrence. Fees for bounced checks/NSF payments can also be added on top if they are spelled out in the lease. Don't try to charge 50% of the rent as a late fee.

7. *Violating tenant's right to privacy and quiet enjoyment of the premises.* Heard of a peeping tom? Don't be that peeping landlord. There are only a reasonable number of instances that a landlord needs to enter the interiors of all units each year. It's fine if the tenant invites the landlord inside the apartment. If the landlord constantly initiates entry, that could be a problem. If there is an accidental entry by a vendor or team member, that is also a problem.

8. *Wrongly using the tenant's security deposit for upgrades and failing to issue an itemized statement.* When it comes to taking a tenant's money, can the before/after condition of the property be proven without a doubt? Can the deductions be proven not to be normal wear & tear? Some landlords expect the apartment to be brand new again, paid by the tenant's deposit, and that assumption is

incorrect. Many items can not be charged for. The landlord still needs to pay for most turnover costs, thus the incentive to renew the existing tenant and avoid vacant units.

9. *Ignoring dangerous conditions (health, life, and safety).* Once the landlord is informed in writing (through the portal), there must be a paper trail where the landlord took swift action (within 24 hours) to rectify the situation. Any evidence of the landlord ignoring a situation or writing it off could result in big headaches for the landlord. Tenants have free legal help available to them.

10. *Not using a rigid set of screening criteria.* These criteria must be set in stone. Anybody interested should receive these criteria. If they meet the criteria, they should tour and apply. If they do not, then they won't be approved. This will save them the $30 application fees, and they will appreciate this. If the landlord does not have any written criteria for screening, then they can be accused of discrimination. Please don't go with "your gut" when you process applications. Act like a robot and use the screening criteria. It's simple. If they pass all the criteria, they are approved.

11. *Failing to have documented procedures according to the law.* It's important to have systems in place for team members to follow. Another team member can fill in if someone doesn't show up for work. Tenants should not have to rely on contacting one specific team member. Anyone from the property management team can meet their immediate needs. Move-ins and move-outs should be a breeze with the same repetitive procedure. Applications, approvals and lease signings happen the same way, every time. Rent payments happen the same way every month.

12. *Code violations with actual fatal results.* For example, the Berkeley, California deck collapse (6 people died when an apartment balcony collapsed) and the "ghost ship fire" (a warehouse blaze that killed 36 people in Oakland, CA). Both of those tragedies were blamed on code violations. Written code violations mean that the property has fallen into serious disrepair. At this point, the landlord is just asking for trouble. They are asking for a lawsuit, or they are asking for someone to get hurt (negligence). Where there is smoke, there's fire. Where there are code violations, there is usually someone behaving badly behind the scenes. When we inherit properties or take over the management of complexes with code violations, the city treats us like criminals. It's important to fix the company's reputation and building ASAP so the bad press does not spread. Even though we didn't do the non-permitted work, we still had a big headache!

13. *Mold Violations.* Mold can be a huge problem for tenants. Mold is very unhealthy to have in an apartment or any structure. It can damage clothing, walls and make the air toxic. Landlords' should act quickly when getting reports of mold. Tenants usually need to stay in hotels while the place gets fixed. Professional mold remediation companies and general contractors should be hired to have a clean paper trail. Otherwise, a tenant could claim the place wasn't remediated properly. Some insurance companies will cover this work.

14. *Lead-Based Paint.* Lead-based paint is a mandatory disclosure. Homes built before 1979 have the possibility of lead-based paint. "Protect Your Family from Lead in Your Home" is a pamphlet

available for download from the EPA (Environmental Protection Agency). They update it frequently. Tenants should be informed of all the possible hazards inside the structure before moving in. Asbestos should also be disclosed, if applicable.

15. *Bed Bugs.* Bed Bugs are a mandatory disclosure. Bed bugs are often carried in through used furniture or clothing. Once they get in, they stay. Tenants must report them ASAP. Treatments are expensive and unavoidable. Do them now before they spread to the neighboring units. We once heard of a complex with 150 of the 300 units infected with bed bugs! Tenants often think it's their problem and expense. Give them comfort that the landlord will pay and eradicate the pests asap.

16. *Prop 65 Signage.* Beware trolling lawyers. These basic signs, which you usually see near the front door of every retailer, need to be posted at your apartment complexes. Post them and sleep better at night. The signs are available online.

17. *Old Safety Railing non-compliant spacing and height.* Again, beware trolling lawyers. Besides the outright safety risk of low banisters and wide guard rails (baluster), there is also a lawsuit risk! Most metal and wood stairs and rails can be retrofitted to be compliant. Keep the existing frame and weld or add-on to make the whole assembly to current safety specifications. A 4-inch sphere should not be allowed to pass through the railing. On some old structures, a basketball could pass through the stair railing! Prevent future tragedies with a small amount of construction today.

18. *Noise/Disturbance affecting other tenants' "safe and quiet enjoyment."* Tenants working from home complain about noise from other tenants more than ever. What is the landlord doing about it? What notices have been sent out to document the disturbances? What proof does one tenant have against the other one? Is there video and audio proof? Have the police been called and a police report filed saying who is at fault? It is important that

the landlord does not play judge and stays impartial. Any noise violation notices should be sent to ALL tenants and not just the one being accused. Always have proof and documentation before jumping to a conclusion. Tenants want peace and quiet. Landlords need to see proof of the violation.

19. *Pool Safety*. Pools must meet strict standards for water quality. Pool fencing must be in good condition to help prevent accidental drowning. Pool surfaces, ladders, safety equipment, signage, and flotation rings, must all be in working order. The pool's surface should not be sharp enough to cut tenants' feet. A drain entrapment device should also be installed (preventing kids' intestines from getting sucked into the filter). Pools should be an amenity, not a hazard.

20. *Pets*. Be clear on your property's pet policy. Service animals are always allowed with current documentation (not expired). Owners of normal pets may be charged a pet deposit. Please consult with your local jurisdiction for the current updated laws. Pets are more prevalent than ever. Pets are companions for many tenants nowadays. The more open a landlord is to pets, the larger the pool of applicants will be for those vacant units. Keep in mind what type of flooring your units have: hard floors are better; carpeted units could have issues from pet stains.

CHAPTER 13

Marketing - How to Get Property Management Clients

Odds are someone in your inner circle probably knows a few landlords. It's best to start off managing a couple of houses first. If the Landlord is not ready to hand over management, then offer to handle the leasing and screening. Once you've established a reputation, landlords will usually hand over full duties to the realtor. It's best to make all the beginner mistakes on a tiny portfolio before taking on 100 doors.

It's very likely someone's aunt or uncle is a landlord. Start within the family first and expand out from there. You can also approach the business from the contracting side; contractors interact daily with landlords! You can tap into that gold mine if you invest in learning the skills.

After forming a business plan, it's just a matter of asking for the business. Start by offering to be the "maintenance manager" before becoming the property manager. Learn the systems from the inside first. Once trust is established with one client, your management portfolio can spread to neighboring buildings and the landlord's friends in an organic way.

Advertising externally is also effective. First, build the management brand. Property management franchises are available, costly and not necessary. Newbies should advertise on all major websites, such as Craigslist.org and Google Adwords. Be sure to target the client's needs. This is not just about putting your pretty face out there.

Send out physical mailers as well. Establish a property management website with search features. If you want to be really aggressive with the guerilla marketing campaign, you can advertise on billboards and city bus wraps. The property management's website should be tenant and landlord friendly.

Align yourself with local businesses like bakeries, dry cleaners, restaurants, golf courses, and grocery stores to establish branding. Install visible, attractive signage on all of the properties under management. Buy a list of contacts and cold-call all of the local apartment owners. Offer landlords a free rent survey in exchange for their email addresses.

Advertise on Facebook with a free, digital offer or an actual "free lunch" for local rental owners if they attend. Advertise in all of the local trade publications. Volunteer to speak at owner meetings. Research online and crash the "meetup groups." Ask the organizer if it's OK to ask for business there first.

Ask the local business brokers and see if there are any management firms for sale. You could even start as an employee of a management firm to get some experience first.

Pay to speak or advertise at local trade shows. Ask realtors and commercial brokers for referral agreements. Many brokers simply want a commission and not management duties. Be sure to assure them that their commissions will not be poached if the owner wants to sell that property in the future.

Get involved with local events such as farmers' markets, charity fundraisers, and art & wine shows. Advertise on supermarket shopping carts. Speak to the head of the five nearest realtor associations. Tell them that you are focusing on property management and want to know what can be done to serve the community of real property owners in their network. Establish yourself as an authority by declaring it repeatedly to everyone in their sphere of influence.

Buy all the books on the market available for property management and absorb the materials as quickly as possible. It is a lot of work, but it's about momentum. Momentum comes from using your energy and building upon the little victories. You will have plenty of failures, but it's important to find out what works, stick with it, and stop spending ad money on methods that don't work.

The great thing about the digital age is the "cost per click," and customer conversion rate is available very quickly! Remember that it now takes more impressions than ever to convert someone to action. Therefore, some of the advertising that is simply for branding should stay online. Before throwing thousands of ad dollars at one vehicle, you should know whether they are going for simple branding vs. immediately meeting the landlord's needs.

CHAPTER 14

Questions to Ask Each New Prospective Client (Apartment Owner)

Getting started and building your brand is very important, and you may experience some bumps and bruises as you navigate your new industry. Eventually, you should be learning from any mistakes and focusing on finding the right "partners" to work with. Here are some examples and actual responses from owners.

Questions to Ask Each New Prospective Client (Apartment Owner)

- What was the reason you became an apartment owner?
- When do you intend to acquire more property?
- What are the immediate concerns?
- Any issues with the existing vendors?
- Are the apartment buildings working for you, or are you working for them?
- How much money MUST you "net" each month?

Here are some questions and actual answers to give you an idea of what to expect. Pay close attention to how each owner responds.

Joe Smith:

- *What was the reason you became an apartment owner?* The property was inherited. I hate real estate.
- *When do you intend to acquire more property?* Never. This is my retirement income.
- *What are the immediate concerns?* I need your team to fill the vacancies ASAP.
- *Any issues with the existing vendors?* I think the plumber is overcharging me.
- *Are the apartment buildings working for you, or are you working for them?* I come here once a week. What do you mean?
- *How much money MUST you "net" each month?* I can survive on the $8,000 this property pays me "net" every month. How much are your management fees going to cost me?

Karen Tom:

- *What was the reason you became an apartment owner?* To create generational wealth for my grandkids. I have six grandkids. Check out their photos.
- *When do you intend to acquire more property?* Well… if the time comes to buy or sell, please let me know if you can handle the listing and purchasing for us.
- *What are the immediate concerns?* Maintaining a 100% occupancy rate and getting the roof replaced.

- *Any issues with the existing vendors?* I want to switch to electronic laundry payments.
- *Are the apartment buildings working for you, or are you working for them?* With your property management in place, I can have so much more free time.
- *How much money MUST you "net" each month?* We take in $10K per month in rent. After expenses, I would expect the "net" to be approximately $7K. Would you like to review last year's income statements that my CPA prepared?

Which client would one prefer to work with? Karen or Joe? Why? On the surface, it appears Karen would be a better client to work with and GROW with. Clients like Joe will probably require more education and hand-holding when complex situations arise. Clients like Karen will also demand that the firm be sophisticated to meet her expectations. Which type of client is your team attracting?

CHAPTER 15

How to Set Fee Rates and Scale Up

This is the part where it's time to earn some money! Scale and grow the business with self-motivated employees and by implementing software. This little property management experiment is actually paying out passive income each month. Some properties now run so efficiently that you might not receive a single service call the entire month—that's called passive income! It's not every month, but *some* months it's passive. The owner still happily pays the property manager.

With your growing client list, the tenants have become too much to manage in your head and smartphone. It's time to sign up for software that can manage your booming business. Software helps to automate so many time-consuming tasks. Monthly reports, maintenance work orders and rent collection are all 100% more efficient through property management software. This allows you to leverage your time to increase your efficiency and effectiveness, leading to happy owners. And happy owners will start referring you to their circle of friends. This is what you are shooting for, right? Think about the average "worker joe." As a wage earner, he or she has one way to earn an income: Every morning, getting up for work and swinging a hammer or sitting in a cubicle for eight hours. If you get sick or injured, you might get paid, maybe not. Property management opens up many more possible income streams.

1. **Management Fees** generally range from 5-10% depending on the size of the apartment complex. A normal fee to charge is 6% for a 10-unit building. Fees are always negotiable. The fees only pertain to collected rents, not scheduled rents. This is an incentive to keep the complexes fully occupied with top-of-market rent.

2. **Leasing Fees.** A normal fee to charge would be 50% of the contract rent. If an apartment rents for $1,000, a leasing fee could be $500. Renewal fees could also be half of the leasing fee.

3. **Remodeling Fees.** If properly licensed, overseeing subcontractors' work can generate fees of 10-15% on top of the construction costs. The job should at least entail full remodeling of at least one unit. Routine maintenance should not have added construction management fees.

4. **Sales Commissions.** Eventually, the old buildings will need to be sold and new buildings purchased. Commissions can be earned when this occurs. A normal commission for selling can be 2.5% for buying and 2.5% for selling. If a $5M building is sold and a $7.5M building is purchased, that will generate a $125,000 fee and $187,500 fee totaling $312,500 in commissions that might take only six months to earn.

5. **Remodeling Jobs.** You can choose to perform remodeling jobs for added profit. Please be sure to be properly licensed, skilled and experienced. Owners can be very picky when it comes to this kind

of work. Be careful and only promise what can be "over-delivered."

Protect the management fees you earn with E&O Insurance, otherwise known as Errors & Omissions insurance. Form a corporation for limited personal liability.

You now have the skills and options to survive and thrive in any economic cycle. Our own business has scaled to the point that my wife even quit her job so she could work with me (or go shopping at the mall!).

Employees work for money. Investors and business owners have their money working for them 24/7. Become a business owner today while you still have the energy and momentum!

CHAPTER 16

Today's Digital World vs. the Old Paper World

Chances are you've attended a virtual meeting through a webcam. Some kids attend classes fully online without any classroom presence (Thanks, COVID!).

This section is about giving up control and learning how to work remotely in this "new world." Like most property managers and rental property owners, I used to think that I was the king of executing the apartment rental process—nobody does it better than me! *How did this building ever run before me!!?* That is simply ego talking, not logic. However, I quickly learned that I could only do so much and keep a high level of professionalism. I had to outsource and start trusting other people. My one-man-band limit was 168 units managed: maintenance, rent collection, reporting, etc. I needed help, but I had to be *willing to accept* a certain percentage of correctable mistakes. Perfection is the enemy of business expansion. You can still take pride in your company's level of growth rather than be satisfied with being flawless and small.

Here's an analogy that everyone can understand. Your friend says, "I *made* a sandwich at home." Did they make the tomato, bread, lettuce, cheese, and meat from scratch? Did they kill the cow and grind the meat? Did they spend hours grinding the flour and proofing the dough? Or did they just pay someone else for all of the ingredients and simply *assemble* the meal? Maybe they just did one essential part—cooked the meat before assembling the food. My point is we have to trust others and outsource what we need *"right now"* to scale our portfolios.

Leverage is absolutely critical to growth. Leverage involves using tools and human resources. The word "lever" is often used to describe a stick that can move a boulder when placed properly. The boulder would not move with just the force of two hands, but with the lever, it began to roll. Once we trust technology and trust those behind the technologies, any growth goal is achievable. Especially now, technology has become a welcome substitute for many tasks related to apartment management.

Some software is even linkable to your bank account. Look at a car manufacturing plant. There is a careful balance between robot assembly machines and human operators. The ultimate goal with leverage is to bring your personnel costs per unit under manageme*nt down a*nd your net profit per unit *up* while expanding your portfolio.

If you still use graph paper, pencil and calculator to manage your rental portfolio, put them down now! There are many software options available. One critical factor to consider is the level of technical support available. Every operator and property management company has a different level of technical and accounting knowledge. For the software to help your business, it needs to work as intended. Let's rephrase that. If property management software is so powerful that it can turn ten hours of work into ten minutes of data entry, but the new employee who needs to use it gets stuck on the accounts payable page for their entire 8-hour shift, that can be frustrating.

On the contrary, when tech support is available via chat and phone, technical roadblocks can be cleared in a matter of minutes rather than slow the whole company's workflow for hours. Another benefit of having cloud-based software is the automatic updates and upgrades. Those days of buying CDs and downloading the software to your desktop and laptop are gone. This new software can be accessed on the go from any mobile phone browser. Select the desktop version, and the software has full functionality anywhere users carry a phone (everywhere there is internet!). For all the reasons listed, the software I recommend is Yardi. There are many property management software solutions available at www.yardi.com

I often get the question, "Why do people really need to meet *face-to-face*? Owners should only meet with other owners, brokers, or managers. Owners should *not* deal with tenants directly. Payroll costs should be directly tied to the level of duties regularly performed. Prospective tenants need to be shown vacant apartments. If you have a resident manager, use this person for that task. If you don't have an onsite manager, consider hiring a leasing agent on hourly wage or commission.

Another way to think about appropriate payroll "cost per task" is through this example. *This* is a warning sign: When a property owner is so busy shopping around for the color of the countertops, emptying the garbage bin in the laundry room, and picking up the cigarette butts on the sidewalk that they miss out on buying a new deal that could have made them millions. When a property owner is personally involved in tasks that are much more appropriate for the management team or vendors, there is nobody available who can substitute for the owner's decisions. Think of it like this; grocery store employees have clearly defined roles. There is a person who fetches the grocery carts in the parking lot. There are multiple cashiers. A fruit and produce person may be stacking 100 oranges neatly into a pyramid. A florist may also be on duty. The butcher in the back cuts and packages the meat. The dairy and refrigerator stockers are heard but not seen. The truck drivers arrive and unload at the loading docks. The maintenance people arrive to fix the leaky roof and then leave. The store manager roams around to various stations based on the intercom calls for help. The assistant manager hovers around the cashiers as they ask for authorization on overcharged or missed items. Now, if the butcher, with his bloody apron, started to fetch the grocery carts in the parking lot, would that seem out of place? If the truck driver arrived at the loading dock and took over the head cashier's job, would that seem strange? Real estate investment and management is a business and should have clearly defined roles as well. This makes every member of the team work together much better. Every gear on a bicycle has a function; if one is off, the bicycle will probably not move when pedaling.

Property owners who self-manage tend to lack the "big picture" view of buying, selling and growing their portfolio. Some property owners buy and own only one investment property their whole lives. Many tasks involved in property management are urgent but not incredibly important. Yes, of course, everything is important. However, "important" decisions are which property to purchase and when to sell. Which plumber to send to fix the leaky toilet is "urgent" but not incredibly "important." In today's digital world, we are constantly bombarded with emails and phone calls. You can prioritize the daily goals with clearly assigned job roles and duties for the team.

When I was general contracting, it was critical for jobs and timelines to be established when the jobs began. Blueprint copies and papers with each subcontractor's job and due date were handed out on day one. By implementing this routine, there were no mistakes or misunderstandings. I learned this lesson the hard way. I initially tried to manage construction jobs with mostly verbal interaction and was left with many jobs half-finished.

For example, the electrical vendor would not continue working until a section of drywall was demolished. The drywall vendor would not be able to hang their sheetrock until more framing was installed. Even though the framing passed inspection, they could not nail drywall onto thin air. The framers needed to come back and install 25% more wood on these walls. The plumbers would not install their vents until the roofer provided the holes and roof jacks. The plumbers wouldn't install the hot tub drain until the foundation crew demolished the concrete slab section under the tub. This turned into a finger-pointing problem with each person claiming, "It's their job to do that, not mine! And I will also need more money because that will be extra work."

Setting clear expectations can seem difficult at first for the beginner. Nobody likes a "know-it-all," and everybody loves an "ask-it-all." Lean on your vendors who might have 30-40 years experience and ask them the best way to go about these processes. Be clear with real estate brokers, lenders, plumbers, handypersons, internal employees and tenants. Again, when a software feature can adequately replace a person on payroll or commission, do it!

All rental applications should be done online through a portal. In the past, collecting a paper application involved meeting up several times, wasting valuable time. Imagine meeting up with a prospect two or three times to collect all of their documents and finding out they are not qualified! That would be 5 to 6 hours of wasted time for both prospect and leasing agent.

Moving in a tenant can also take a long time. Signing a lease electronically is widely accepted now. How many of us remember going in person to sign three copies of the lease each time? First, block out three hours on your calendar. Then print three paper sets, then staple, then highlight each field. You also better hope there are no typos, or else it's time to grab the Wite-Out and a typewriter! Just in case, print out three blank lease copies and bring those in your briefcase. Bring three blue pens and get to the apartment early. After two people arrive, the third is late, stuck in traffic. This gives the two people already there time to walk around the apartment and nitpick about everything that was already old before they move in.

Maybe you enjoy "shooting the breeze" with people for hours without purpose. Even worse is faxing a lease back and forth four times because nobody can read it. The lease paper looks like it was dropped in water before the dog ate it.

The better way to sign a lease is through an electronic service. If you don't know how to do this, hire someone. You can't afford not to. Once the lease is uploaded and signed electronically, all assigned parties receive a copy (tenants often ask for a copy of their lease when all they have to do is to search their email inbox). Then upload their lease, driver's license, other accompanying documents, paystub, etc., into their tenant file in the portal. In the future, any renewals, rent increases, or notices can also be thrown into the tenant file in the digital "cloud." Don't trust the cloud? Well, I guess some people still store their life savings in the coffee can in the cabinet. Yes, it's time to move away from the can.

Digital locks are commonly available at home improvement stores now. Once the tenant has paid all of their move-in funds, provide the tenant with their unique access code. Eliminate the wasted payroll hours waiting to meet a tenant while they are stuck in traffic. Are there properties and employees that live an hour apart? That would take one hour to drive to the property, one hour to meet & greet, then another hour to drive home. How many times has a tenant "misplaced" their keys inside the apartment or accidentally locked the bottom knob when they went across the hall to the laundry room? Digital locks all but eliminate those "oops" moments.

Another way to handle the lockouts is by implementing and enforcing tenant penalties. Make the tenant call a locksmith because they will get there sooner than a roaming leasing agent ever could. Charge a $75 lockout fee. It's highly doubtful any tenant will forget their keys somewhere after they have paid a locksmith once. Call this policy "tenant tuition," just like late fees. A digital lock is a much better permanent solution that puts no pressure on either party. Change the code when the senior roommate graduates and the sophomores remain in the unit. Train the tenants to understand and *not ignore* the low battery warning alerts that occur every 9 to 12 months. Tenants also love to arrive on their own sweet schedule without having appointments. If the tenant hasn't reached out on their own within a couple of days, check in with them to see if anything needs to be tuned up.

What is the best way to serve notices to tenants? Printing paper and applying pieces of tape to each door in the wind/rain/snow doesn't sound appealing? There is a better method—digitally.

Use the digital tools available for something like a water shutoff or notice of exterior pressure washing or painting. Property management software can send one-click emails to all tenants with attachments, photos, etc. These emails are private and singular, meaning that all 200 tenants will receive the email but won't see the email addresses of the other 199 tenants. The email will appear as a 1:1 email between two people.

However, when there is a serious legal case such as eviction, follow the local legislation requiring paper vs. digital notices allowed in court. To state the obvious, do not text 60 tenants individually or on a group chat. When there is a choice, push all communication through the management software portal.

Online rent collection benefits:

- *Automatic Rent Collection.* Stop being a debt collector and let the software collect rents every month. The most important function of any property management company or owner-operator is to collect the rent. Software is open for collection 24 hours a day, 7 days a week. If old School tenants want to pay with cash? No problem, get those tenants a barcode, and they can pay at a local convenience store. Tech-savvy tenants can set up autopay for their bank account every month. Roommates can figure out their splits and get paid automatically every month on a specific day (after payday). Stop accepting payments through the mail via paper check or money order/cashier's check. There is a small processing fee that the tenant has to pay. Stamps, envelopes and gas to the post office cost money, so the fee is nominal. Credit cards can also be used as a payment option. Guarantors may also get registered and make rent payments for their dependents. All of those old stories about landlords knocking on every door and asking for money can still be true. However, if you want to make the best use of time, forget that method. All repetitive processes should be automated if you are thinking of expanding your unit count or running a professional management outfit. Only place payroll activities for jobs that require a human factor. Do you want to handle a stack of cash or checks and then spray each bill with sanitizer? For the inherited tenants who resist converting to digital payments or any service fee, just explain that a lost check fee or losing a money order would be far more costly. When tenants pay, they get an instant receipt that their payment is posted. When the COVID-19 lockdowns started and the economy came to a grinding halt, 4 out of 5 local bank branches were closed or only open a few hours per day. With automated rent collection, there is no fear or worry about "making it to the bank before 5 p.m." in rush hour traffic! Imagine how hard it would be if you were still collecting 500 paper check rents (x 5 roommates in each apartment = 2,500 paper checks) and hand carrying the bundles to each bank twice daily! How easy is it to lose one check or write a deposit receipt incorrectly (one number typo)? Bank tellers also make mistakes. Tenants often write the wrong payee on the check. Let's take human error out of the equation completely.

- *Going Fully Paperless.* You might remember putting together manual rent rolls every month, saving them, and emailing them to clients. The client would make changes and email them back to me. Three days later, everybody had either version 2.3 or 2.5b with their new changes. Online documents helped a little bit and also lacked the live data feed when new rents came in the next day. Think about the way that it used to be. When a paper rent check came in, three copies of the check were made, each put in the appropriate folder. *Then* the rent was recorded on the excel spreadsheet. *Then* the back of the check got stamped with the account info (it was time-saving back then!). *Then* the deposit slip gets filled out and set aside until more checks come in to make a trip worthwhile. *Three hours later,* you're back home from the bank with the deposit receipt. *Then* you pull out the crumpled receipt and staple the receipt to the correct check copy. *Then* you wait for the paper bank statement to arrive to make sure the funds went into the correct account. Wow! That was a lot of manual labor for just one rent payment! Now, with paperless rent collection, just look at the automatic digital reports to see where the money is. No more trips to the bank to deposit rent checks, except to drop laundry coins. However, those are all being converted to digital payments as well. Laundry coin box thefts have become too frequent with no prosecution. With digital collection and empty coin boxes, nothing is tempting the thieves.

- *Automated Expenses.* Expenses should all be paid via autopay or billpay. Software can also integrate billpay. At the end of the month, the payments get reconciled. Any spikes in usage can be disputed. The inefficient method is to wait for each bill in the traditional mail, hand write a check and walk it down to the post office. Why waste so much time with routine expenses? Spend time reviewing the vendor repair bills, not the utility bills.

- *Monthly Reporting.* Back in the day, one would have to PDF each report page, package them together and email them to clients individually, hoping there were no typos or miscalculations. Property management software simply generates reports, and in approximately 60 seconds, the reports are sent in bulk to all clients. That's right! The monthly reports are *done in 60 seconds!* These monthly reports can even be sent from a mobile phone (no app needed) using the desktop version of any web browser. Cloud software technology is incredible because it's always updated to the latest version. No waiting for the newest version of the software to arrive by CD. 20 hours of laser-focused, "do not interrupt me" time previously spent on monthly reports can now be compressed into 60 seconds. Sounds too good to be true? Most companies offer free demo sessions for prospective subscribers.

Use technology to leverage time by implementing auto-response email and text messages. Funnel leads to the correct department (leasing/management/sales/maintenance), so payroll cost is appropriately applied.

Hire a virtual assistant or automated assistant with a "1-800" number. Have all calls routed to the employee on duty. All media and advertising should be consistent with the same team phone number and email address. When employees leave, there is no need to change the advertising information. The company will not skip a beat.

CHAPTER 17

Forms Glossary and Useful Information

These forms are intended to save time and reduce errors in business operations. Imagine typing these from scratch or memory every time someone requests a list! Any processes that can be automated where there are numerous repetitive inquiries should be standardized within your company. Employees should not put their "spin" on the move-in/move-out process. These are not legal documents. Please follow your area's local laws and regulations.

Onboarding list from new clients:

	List of Items needed from new clients
#	Description
1	Set of Keys
2	Soft Copy of all Leases & most recent rent increase
3	Any House Rules Addenda for Lease Documents

4	Schedule of Arrears, if any
5	Rent Roll & Security Deposit Schedule
6	List of Owner's Immediate Concerns
7	Agreed start date, ideally 30 days in the future
8	Interior and Exterior inspection of all units with Owner
9	Location of all building shutoff valves (water main, etc.)
10	Location of all cleanouts, timers, photocells, meters
11	Existing Vendor List
12	Neighboring Owner contact list, if any
13	Signed Management Agreement PMA

Rental and application information

Here is a sample email that can be sent to all prospects interested in a tour or applying.

Thanks for your interest in renting the property.

Step 1: When you apply on the portal as a group, please apply together and fill out 100% of the information required for screening.

Step 2: Please provide the following documents by email to yours@gmail.com

- Recent job pay stubs for all adults
- Bank Statement Balance for all adults (do not show the account number, just the balance) showing at least 6 months (rent+deposit+utilities) in reserve funds.
- Driver's License/passport photos
- Any pets - regular (breed restrictions) or service animals?
- No smoking?
- Confirm your move-in date and lease expiration date.
- 700 minimum credit score is required. Please inquire about all the rental criteria if you are unsure.

Rental Criteria:

1. 3.5x Rent = Gross income
2. 700 credit score or higher
3. No bankruptcy, eviction
4. Good landlord history
5. No criminal record
6. Employment history
7. Co-signer if applicable
8. No Smoking
9. Pets: each property is different. Please inquire

Thanks for your interest in renting the property.

Form above explained

Step 1: When you apply on Rentcafe.com as a group, please apply together and fill out 100% of the information required for screening.

Some prospects assume that each person can apply separately, or some can apply first and then be added later. A prospect might wrongly assume that only their cosigner or the spouse who has a credit history needs to apply. It's important to help make the process smooth for all staff and prospects who turn into tenants.

Step 2: Please provide the following documents by email to yours@gmail.com

Credit and background checks are part of the equation. The prospect must prove all that they claim on the application is current and valid.

1. *Recent job pay stubs for all adults.* Employment must be verified to ensure timely rent payments.

2. *Bank Statement Balance for all adults (do not show the account number, just the balance) Showing at least 6 months (rent+deposit+utilities) in reserve funds.* Prospects who need $5,000 in move-in funds but show $875 in their checking accounts might need a cosigner or simply be denied.

3. *Driver's License/passport photos.* Verifying identity and past addresses is key to double checking the background check for errors.

4. *Any pets - regular (breed restrictions) or service animals?* Some properties may allow pets with certain rules like maximum pounds or maximum two pets or increased deposit and pet rent.

5. *No smoking?* Most properties are non-smoking now, and it's good practice to get this confirmed from the prospects upfront.

6. *Confirm your move-in date and lease expiration date.* Many times prospects will just quickly click through the application with the move-in defaulting as today when they actually desire to move in two to four weeks with a 6 to 24-month term. This information needs to be confirmed upfront to avoid multiple edits to the lease.

7. *700 minimum credit score is required. Please inquire about all the rental criteria if you are unsure.* Credit score is probably the most important factor that determines the likelihood that rent will be paid on time. There may be some scenarios where a prospect has a limited credit history and no late payments or collections, but their score is under 700. It's up to management's discretion if they want to make an exception. There can also be applicants that come up as a "no-match" in the system meaning that they don't have a valid social security number or there is a typo. This is why having the current address and driver's license information can also be enough to pull up credit information.

Rental Criteria:

It's critical that these criteria are 100% identical for each prospect. Otherwise, it's a fair housing violation. Whatever criteria are established apply to everyone interested in the vacancies. The only exception may be tenants with a subsidy or voucher program. Those tenants should still be required to have a high credit score and be able to pay their portion of the voucher easily.

For example, if the rent is $2,000 per month and the government pays $1,700 per month, the tenant should make at least $1,200 per month. Again the rules just need to be consistent, and there are plenty of housing voucher candidates with good credit. Approving an unqualified prospect when a landlord is desperate to fill the space often ends poorly.

Message that is sent with every lease document

//Insert this message below into every electronic envelope sent out for signatures//

Welcome to the Property =)

Please see the enclosed electronic lease. Review, then click to sign when ready. You will receive a completed copy.

The next steps will be

- Sign Lease
- Pay move-in funds thru your portal
- Setup a time for keys transfer
- Transfer Electric & Gas utilities into your name
- Move in & get settled
- Let us know any items that need attention

Warmest Regards,
Mgmt

Form above explained

//Insert this message below into every electronic envelope sent out for signatures//

1. *Welcome to the Property =).* Tenants love to get a nice greeting. Feel free to add an emoji.
2. *Please see the enclosed electronic lease. Review, then click to sign when ready. You will receive a completed copy.* Tenants want to make sure they will get a copy and can locate that digital file easily in the future.
3. *The next steps will be*
   - *Sign Lease.* All tenants have to sign it to be completed.
   - *Pay move-in funds through your portal.* Encourage tenants to pay a few days early so funds can post.
   - *Setup a time for keys transfer.* Whether this is a door code or physical keys, just specify the process, whether it is contact-free or an appointment is required.
   - *Transfer Electric & Gas utilities into your name.* Send a link if needed.
   - *Move in & Get Settled.* Congratulate the new tenant!
   - *Let us know any items that need attention.* Be sure to send the maintenance crew promptly after receiving the tune-up list. Let the tenant know the property will not be remodeled while occupied and maintenance will gladly be handled.

Warmest Regards,
Mgmt

Sample parking & storage diagram

Parking/Storage Diagram			
StorageLocker	Parking Spot	Apt	Vehicle Make/Model/Plate
1	A	1	Honda/Accord/789ert4
2	B	2	Honda/Accord/789ert4
3	C	3	Honda/Accord/789ert4
4	D	4	Honda/Accord/789ert4
5	E	5	Honda/Accord/789ert4

Tenants have a tendency to park in the vacant unit spots and take up visitor spaces when the area is high density. The property management firm must enforce the parking assignment map and tow the violators. All spots must be clearly marked with paint on the asphalt or labeled numbers or letters overhead.

Some new tenants will assume that their apartment number or letter equals their parking space. Always put the correct space in the lease to avoid disputes after move-in and provide a parking map. It needs to be clear. You don't want a tenant who moves into apartment #1 to assume their spot is the garage space labeled #1 when their assigned space is #15, an uncovered space next to the garbage bin. If one tenant parks in the wrong spot, this creates a negative domino effect where all of the residents learn that they need just to grab any open space; "If nobody else is following the rules, then why should I?" It doesn't take long for every tenant in this complex to be mad and calling the property management firm to complain! Enforce the rules and tow when necessary. The tenants that see other cars get towed will never "accidentally" forget their correct parking spot.

Sample phone scripts with the PM (property manager) and prospects with possible responses you may receive.

PM: How many people will be living in the unit?

Prospect: 3

PM: Adults and children all count. Is it 3 total occupants?

Prospect: 3 adults and 3 kids.

PM: This is a two-bedroom apartment, and the maximum is 5 people. You will need to have a three-bedroom apartment. Let me check if we have any available.

Prospect: I meant 3 adults and 2 kids. 5 total.

PM: Let me do some research and text you back with some options.

The prospect may be trying to circumvent your rules by changing their story to fit your requirements. That's a huge red flag. If the prospect had said five or fewer occupants initially, then continue.

PM: Any Pets?

Prospect: Yes, we have a dog; he is nice.

PM: Is it a service animal?

Prospect: No, just our pet.

PM: No pets are allowed at this property. Sorry.

Prospect: Actually he is a service animal. I can send you the paperwork.

PM: No problem, they are welcome.

PM: Good credit above 700 is required. What is your estimated score?

Prospect: I don't know my credit score, but it's probably OK.

PM: It would be a good idea to check your credit score online or with your credit card company before you see the place, as the owner is pretty strict on this requirement. Let me know what you can find out.

Prospect: I want to see the place first.

PM: If you are unsure of your score range, please check your credit score first.

PM: We require a certain gross monthly income to qualify (3.5 x Rent = GMI). What's your estimated gross monthly income?

Prospect: I have cash income, not W-2. Can I still apply?

PM: Can you provide bank statements with proof of deposits? A signed letter from your employer? A copy of your tax return?

Prospect: I have a housing voucher. How can I meet this income requirement?

PM: Credit score is more important than income in your case. Please make sure your credit does not have any major dings, and you can apply in the portal. If you know your portion of the rent, you would still need to make sufficient income to pay your portion every month. If your portion is $250 out of the total $2,000 in rent, you would need to make $875 per month (3.5x the $250). Please show proof from your current landlord that your portion is $250.

PM: What's your desired move-in date?

Prospect: In around three weeks or so.

PM: We would like the move-in date to be ASAP to 4 weeks from now (any future move-in dates should be revisited later).

PM: Do you prefer a Ground Floor or Second Floor?

Prospect: It needs to be ground level and facing southeast.

PM: # of Bedrooms Needed?

Prospect: Two.

PM: # of Bathrooms Needed?

Prospect: One.

PM: # of Assigned Parking Spaces Needed?

Prospect: Two.

PM: Laundry in Unit needed (yes/no)?

Prospect: Yes, needed.

PM: When are you and all of your occupants available to see the apartment (together)?

Prospect: Saturday at 1 p.m.

PM: Virtual Tour/FaceTime/Can one person decide for the group?

Prospect: Yes, David can decide for the group.

Following a predetermined phone script and sticking to the questions is important since you will encounter all types of prospects with every answer imaginable. Without these rigid screening procedures, confusion and clarity issues can arise between the leasing agent and the prospect. Here are some examples of unhappy prospect comments after a pre move-in screening was not done.

- "The unit was upstairs, and I need a downstairs unit because my leg is broken."
- "You didn't tell me that children count for the occupancy limit. We have six people for a one-bedroom apartment, but only three adults."
- "I only wanted to see units with laundry, and this place only has a shared laundry room."
- "I love the place, and I forgot to tell you that I have three "regular pet" dogs. Is that allowed?"
- "I wanted a place with two bathrooms, not just one. Isn't that what you told me?"
- "This front door doesn't face southeast. That was my number one concern."
- "I cook a lot, so only a gas stove will work for me. This one has electric. Yuck."
- "I will only rent the apartment if you remodel it entirely first."
- "I thought this was a three-bedroom apartment, and it's a two-bedroom plus den."

As you can see, most if not all of those issues would have been avoided if the tenant's concerns and the property manager's requirements were clearly covered in the pre move-in screening.

How to handle non-emergency repair requests

1. The tenant submits a work order through the portal.
2. Refer to the approved Vendor list regarding who to set up for this job.
3. Give Tenant Vendor info and Vendor Tenant info. Let them schedule the work.

4. Follow up in a few days to see if it's done yet. Email/Text. Do not call as it takes too much time.
5. Ask any necessary questions along the way.

Apartment Entry Rules and Regulations for leasing and maintenance personnel

1. Never enter an apartment until you are absolutely sure it's clear.
2. Check with the manager first. Verify approved entry with the owner.
3. When onsite, knock two times and wait. Knock again.
4. No response from knocking? Call the last number on file.
5. Never been in the unit before? Call the manager again.
6. Sometimes, a tenant needs to be moved out in the leasing software so new apps can be submitted. However, the tenant might still be living there. Please make a sheet for these discrepancies.
7. If unsure or unconfirmed… simply do not enter!
8. The owner may not have updated the manager 100%. Always exercise caution.
9. As a rule, *do not show* occupied units. If someone wants to break their lease, tenants may show their own unit.
10. If you enter an apartment without permission or an appointment, you are responsible for the consequences (you may enter on someone who is naked or compromised—instant lawsuit! Or worse, you can be lawfully shot).

When in doubt, cancel the showing. It can wait. The safety and privacy of our existing tenants are more important than anything. Follow these rules above, and we will all be safe.

"How to break your lease" notice for tenants

Please refer to your lease. This is just a supplemental guide and not legal advice.

Introduction: Landlord understands that things happen, and tenants may want to get out of their lease. Please read below and then contact us with your preference so we can work with you.

Contract Points:

1. Tenant is responsible for payments due through the end of the contract lease term.

2. Security deposit is not applied to your "rent due" prior to move-out.

Options available to you:

1. Prepay the remainder of the lease, then move out.

Example: Tenant lease expires on May 31st. Tenant moves out on May 1st. Payment for May rent is still due.

2. Existing Tenant to find a suitable sublease tenant, "new roommate," to join the existing tenant on the lease. Ask friends or co-workers. New roommate must meet the application standards of the landlord: 700 credit score, income, landlord history, no criminal records, etc. Landlord will not show the apartment while it is still occupied. Showings and advertisements are up to the tenant.

Example: Existing tenant has a co-worker that would like to be added to the lease. If their application is approved and their credit score is above 700, but their income is not enough, this is the best solution. Existing tenants may physically move out but stay on the lease due to income or other qualifying requirements.

3. Existing tenant to find a replacement tenant for the remainder of the term. New Occupants must meet application standards of the landlord: 700 credit score, income, landlord history, no criminal records, etc. Landlord will not show the apartment while it is still occupied. Showings and advertisements are up to the tenant.

Example: Existing tenant has a co-worker that would like to take over their apartment until the lease expires. If their application is approved and they plan to move out after the lease expires, this is the best option.

4. Existing tenant finds a new tenant to sign a new 1-year lease agreement. New Occupants must meet application standards of the

landlord: 700 credit score, income, landlord history, no criminal records, etc. Landlord will not show the apartment while it is still occupied. Showings and advertisements are up to the tenant.

Example: A new tenant who is approved may sign a new lease that begins at an agreed upon date before the current tenant's lease expiration date.

5. You move out and then we place an ad for rent. You're responsible for payments until the new tenant we find moves in (not beyond your lease expiration).

If the new tenant moves in after your lease expires, the previous tenant is still responsible for payments through your lease expiration.

Example 1: Existing tenant moves out on April 1st. Existing tenant's lease expires on July 1st. Landlord places an ad on April 1st, Landlord approves a new tenant to move in on May 1st. Existing tenant is relieved of responsibility for May and June rent payments.

Example 2: Existing tenant moves out on April 1st. Existing tenant's lease expires on July 1st. Landlord places an ad on April 1st, Landlord approves a new tenant to move in on June 15th. Existing tenant is relieved of responsibility for two weeks of rent payments.

6. If you simply move out, you are responsible for payments due through the end of your lease term. If you do not pay, your credit report will be negatively affected. It will be better for you if you work with us.

7. Security Deposit deductions for the damages in the apartment still apply. Refer to your lease.

8. Outgoing tenant is still responsible for their lease obligations until the incoming tenant signs their lease and pays their security deposit and move-in rent. At that point, the incoming tenant can no longer back out and we can agree on a date to release the outgoing tenant from their lease obligations.

How many people are allowed per unit?

Unit Occupancy Fair Housing Federal Guidelines

- 2 per bedroom + 1 extra person
- Adults and children all count as one person
    - 1 bedroom = 2+1 = 3 maximum
    - 2 bedroom = 4+1 = 5 maximum
    - 3 bedroom = 6+1 = 7 maximum
    - 4 bedroom = 8+1 = 9 maximum

Etc.

Applications for more people than is allowed per unit type will not be accepted.

No Smoking Policy

Friendly reminder: This is a "no-smoking" property. There is no smoking allowed on the premises. Residents and guests must adhere to this policy. If you see anybody smoking on the property, please report to management ASAP. Violators will be served written notice to comply. Thanks for your cooperation in keeping this property smoke-free.

Management

Tenant Frequently Asked Questions (FAQ)

Before you promise a prospect anything you are not 100% sure about, all you have to say is, "I will check on that and get back to you."

Otherwise, if certain amenities are promised and not delivered, someone has to do damage control and it looks very bad on our part. It looks like we are either misinformed or doing a bait & switch—not good. The "golden rule" is to simply say, "I don't know." Please don't pretend you are the owner and make all the rules. Each property has quirks and unique features.

Examples of tenant questions and appropriate PM responses:

- *Where is my parking spot- is it a carport or open?* "I will check on that and get back to you regarding the specific location of parking assignments and if they are free or cost a monthly fee. How many cars do you have?"

- *What utilities are included with the rent?* "I will check on that and get back to you." *Most, not* all, properties include water, sewer, and garbage with the rent. However, you may have one property that includes storm drain and *not* Sewer. That distinction is important. *Some* properties have common utilities that are either *fixed* or *variable*. Ask the Owner first before promising anything. It is perfectly appropriate to say, "I am new to this property. I can show you the apartment. However, I don't know the answer. Let me ask and get back to you ASAP."

- *Is renters insurance required?* "Yes, for all properties, with pet coverage if you have a pet."

- *Are pets allowed?* "What kind of pets do you have? We have breed restrictions. I will check on that and get back to you."

- *What are the move-in specials, and can you do any better?* "What is your move-in date? You will also need to apply first before we can promise you any deal. That is our policy."

- *I am actually looking for an upstairs unit. Can you show me another one now?* "Let me double check if we have any upcoming vacancies, and we can make another appointment."

- *Can you do a three-month lease?* "I will check on that and get back to you."

- *Can I move in today?* "It usually takes three days to get you approved, paid up and moved in."

- *How many machines are in the laundry room?* "I can show you now, or I will check on that and get back to you." FYI: *Not* every property has laundry!

- *Is my unit going to have AC or in-unit laundry?* "I will check on that and get back to you."

CHAPTER 18

Case Studies

Case Study 1

- 2017 Presidents day holiday we had a local heat wave.
- 7-plex in Menlo Park, CA, the owner called me in a panic on Sunday. The electrical meter for one unit had blown up.
- All the electricians in town were not available
- Through my network, I was able to get them back in service within one hour.
- Total bill was $21K with a $2k insurance deductible.

Lesson learned: Treat your vendors well, pay on time, and have at least four in each construction category. Note in your journals which ones work nights and weekends. It *will* matter when one is not ready!! Having a relationship with the vendor means that one might have stored cell phone numbers of the owner when the office line is not picking up.

Case Study 2

We got information from the client before we took over management. This hassle pushed the owner over the edge to ask for help.

- Townhouse-style unit up and down. There was a water leak from the shower upstairs that resulted in mold.
- Tenant refused access to review and perform repairs.
- Tenant got mold testing and then claimed sickness from the mold. They tried to get neighbors to claim also.
- Tenant hired an attorney to instruct no direct communication or attempt to enter.
- Tenant did not pay rent for four months under an uninhabitable claim.

- The judgment for the tenant was a $44k settlement.
- Insurance paid 50%; the owner paid 50%.

Silver lining: After a $6k remodel, the unit was rented after just one day on the market for $600 more per month than the previous lease.

Case Study 3

- Hoarding tenant. Married, then divorced. Living alone. Mental health deteriorated. Gradually accumulated more items.
- Rent paid by his parents.
- Tenant moved in six homeless people.
- Homeless people claimed they had a lease.
- Tenant claimed maintenance issues were not fixed.
- Access physically impossible, garbage piled up high.

- Police called twice. They would not get involved but helped to give tenants a reality check.
- Tenants a "no show" at the court date.
- Sheriff issued a lockout.
- Door was removed while the tenant was allowed three hours to remove their belongings.

Lesson learned: Always inspect the property interiors at least two times per year. Encourage all tenants to report issues without fear of retaliation from the neighbors. Unfortunate situations like this illustrate the importance of good legal advice. There were so many issues happening here. Tenants have rights whether or not they pay rent or have a lease. Please do not make up your own rules when you come into a situation like this. Always follow the local laws.

CHAPTER 19

There Is No Such Thing as a Management-Free-Forever Asset

Management and owner involvement with a property can't be avoided, only delayed for years or outsourced. Even Triple Net (NNN - in addition to the rent, the tenant pays for building maintenance, insurance and property taxes). Properties eventually require management and tough decisions to be made.

Please see below what happened to a retired apartment investor who bought a NNN property:

A past client was fed up with managing apartments, reached their breaking point and traded out of local apartments to an out-of-state NNN. Triple net retail as an exit from apartments is an acceptable trade as long as the building stays occupied.

The NNN tenant paid rent without fail for 10 years until…

The corporate tenant did not renew, and the *empty* building is now worth half the original purchase price. The value of the building now sank to its reconstruction/replacement (much lower) cost instead of the value of the lease payments (much higher).

NNN properties generally do not appreciate; value is entirely lease dependent. The simplest way to explain this is valuing a car based on who the driver is, not the car. Developers make the most profit on these NNN deals.

NNN property is rented above market rate with the tenant paying back the tenant improvement allowance when vacant property could be worth 50% of the original purchase price.

If you must buy a retail or office property, make sure the current rents are *at* or *below* market rate. Otherwise, there is a risk that the investor will be shocked when the tenant vacates.

When owning a 10-unit apartment building, 1 vacancy is only 10% vacant. It's no big deal when tenants move in and out because it usually means the new rent you can charge is more than the last occupant.

Single tenant equals 100 percent vacancy or 100 percent occupancy. It's all or nothing. If you like playing roulette in the casino, this is the right property for you.

Significant tenant improvements and exterior refresh work are usually required to attract a new tenant. The cost of tenant improvements could easily shock any investor. Small investment buildings could cost $10/SF, which is no joke. To top it off, those improvements will probably be outdated when the tenant vacates. On the other hand, that old apartment could remain unrenovated and appear to a variety of tenants for 40 years straight.

Don't blame the property; blame the process or pattern for the headache created. The same apartment complex can be a headache for one owner and a blessing for another. Why is that? The key is property management.

Hire a manager instead of changing property type. If the goal is cash flow, show the apartment owner how to meet their cash flow needs without taking on any more debt or reducing their equity by the commission price. Convince them to secure professional property management and relieve the burden of self-operating.

Stay within a multi-family type; everyone needs a place to live. The economic cycles will drive rents up and down. At the end of the day, everyone should be reasonably diversified. An apartment building that is paid off can be one of the best and safest performing assets you can own.

The retail landscape is changing and unpredictable. For example, Amazon, Walgreens, Walmart, etc., can take out any small fast food or grocery franchise. What was once a seemingly safe fast food NNN could become obsolete within five years. How safe of an investment was a Borders Bookstore just a few years ago? Haven't heard of them lately? EXACTLY!!

Why choose apartments vs. NNN properties? The answer is simple: Apartments are a pandemic and recession-proof asset. Everyone needs housing. Everyone does not need a fast food restaurant on every corner, which can close at any time. What if there is a lawsuit regarding one of the restaurant's toxic ingredients? They could go bankrupt overnight.

Multi-family assets income increases with inflation (subject to rent control), and vacancies are easily filled without much tenant improvement. Everyone needs a place to live. What other reasons can you think of to join the apartment industry?

CHAPTER 20

When to Say "No" (What to Avoid)

With Owners:

- When the proper

- Property is too small to make a profit for your firm—just say, "No."

- When the requests are too demanding—just say, "No."

- When the owner refuses to provide working capital for long-term capital improvements—just say, "No. There is too much potential liability from damages due to properties in disrepair.

- When owners only want one to rent out their house—just say, "No." We only provide full-service management because the leasing portion of the management fees is often a non-profitable activity. It is absolutely essential to management, but the real long-term profits come from long-term management with high occupancy rates and very few turnovers.

- Just say "no" to different processes from each owner. If you want to scale larger, the onboarding process for each owner needs to be identical. As long as profits are maximized, existing owners will accept a uniform system. Make this change as quickly as possible. What does this mean? Full-service management means that all aspects and decisions of the management are the responsibility of the PM. Important decisions should still be made together in writing with the owner. Owners may provide their preferences with the level of involvement, but they are not allowed to slow down the processes. For example, if an owner wants to pay all monthly vendor invoices but questions them down to the last detail, that can be a problem. Pretty soon, the vendors will complain about not getting paid on time. However, I've learned over time that most owners want to be less and less involved. Just send them the draw on schedule every month. The role of a PM is to allow the owner to save net money each month and have more free time; remember that when negotiating with vendors. If the owner can do a better job and they still have the energy, that is a deciding factor.

- Just say "no" to working for free. If the original PM contract does not include all the current duties, then call the owner to discuss market-adjusted compensation. It's important to over-deliver on services provided within the boundaries of one's duty. The goal of every property manager should be to create raving clients that refer business to their friends and family.

- Just say "no" to working for less than the market rate. Plenty of owners will try to "lowball" a fee estimate. As much as robots and software can help to manage processes, the industry is still widely operated by humans. Humans require payroll, insurance, 401k, medical, etc. For example, the worst thing you can agree to is a 3% management fee when the market is collecting an 8% management fee. If the property ends up being a headache, it might actually cost more to manage than the fees earned.

- When an owner becomes abusive—just say, "No."

With Tenants:

- Just say "no" to abusive tenants. Always treat tenants (and owners) as professionals. Friends can be full-service. However, business must come first. If there is any harassment from tenants (or owners), that behavior must be corrected as soon as possible before it becomes a pattern.

- Just say "no" to tenants who demand that you set appointments, make revisions and give "by-the-hour" updates on the plumber's arrival. The last thing you want to be is a secretary and travel agent for the tenants. The only way to scale one's business is to have a healthy ratio of team members to units under management. The more non-revenue producing duties a team member has, the more wasted payroll hours are spent. The best thing you can do is lift the burden of scheduling off team members and put the burden on the tenant and vendor. Make sure to clearly state that the financial responsibility still lies with the property management firm. Some tenants wrongly assume that if they have to call the appliance company, they have to pay for the refrigerator repair bill. The property management company must simply explain that the tenant only needs to provide their availability and call the vendor directly for all updates. The management company will handle all billing directly with the vendor. This will benefit the tenant in receiving faster service and subsequent updates.

With Vendors:

- Just say "no" to vendors who refuse to follow the rules. Vendors who cause tenants to complain for reasons such as being ineffective, talking rudely, or missing appointments should be replaced.

- Just say "no" to using vendors that are too cheap to be true. When the author was a general contractor, there were four main ready-mix concrete suppliers. This is the type of concrete that comes "wet and ready to pour" with an expiration time. The prices per yard were all within 10 percent of each other. However, there was one cheaper supplier that had a deserved reputation for cracking more frequently. If a contractor wanted to make 5% more profit on a job but risked having to redo the whole job they went with the cheaper supplier. It makes more sense to go with the slightly higher priced supplier and avoid headaches down the line.

Other times it is OK to say No:

- Refusing to take on problem properties will help your business stay lean and efficient. Problematic properties are the biggest time drain on employee cost ratios.

- The biggest mistake you can make is taking a property outside of your coverage area. New property managers and realtors usually make this mistake. *How can you say no to $$$?* Yes, but the money will probably have a short-term benefit. Will it help your local portfolio?

- Perhaps a family member or existing client convinces you to manage a small property that is *only* a 10-hour drive away. Don't worry, "It won't be much work." Once you agree, you are stuck finishing the job. Knowing your limits in advance and refusing this account does not mean that you can't assist the client. You can still lookup the local property management companies in that town and call them for pre-interviews. Then recommend the top three firms to your client. You have politely refused while helping them at the same time. If anything goes wrong, three companies were recommended.

- Just say "no" to supervising unfamiliar or new jobs. Agreeing to oversee the complete remodeling of a building facade without any experience could end up a disaster. *Don't* fake it until you make it. If your current experience with remodeling only involves painting and carpet cleaning, just be upfront with the client. A maintenance expert must be called in for training or project management. The last thing you should do is try to general contract the big remodel job and get the sequence wrong. Then you have to explain why the stucco needs to be redone, and the owner needs to pay double the initial budget. Your job as a PM is to save the owner money on maintenance and capital improvements. It's critical to have the tough conversations upfront about money "well spent" (higher rents) and money that could be "easily spent" but does not raise rents or building values.

- Just say "no" to clients who want you to "lowball" vendors and service providers. Asking for a 10 to 15 percent discount with exclusive rights or a volume contract is good and advisable. Good vendors are hard to come by. The best owners in the area all use the same vendors. Therefore, patience and politeness are required. Rarely are talented vendors "hungry for work" standing outside a hardware store. They are usually just trying to figure out which work order is more urgent and more profitable. The vendor will attend to those first. Always pay the vendor immediately upon finishing the job. Offer generous deposits to start the job. Use the same vendors over and over to develop long-term relationships. Buying lunches and gift cards go a long way. Our vendor team always answers our phone calls. Weekdays and weekends are no issue.

- Just say "no" to overloading vendors. Make sure the vendor can handle the work order volume and does outstanding work. For example, a toilet fixed poorly for $150 may break again two weeks later and cost $200 more to fix for a total of $350. On the other hand, a toilet fixed properly may cost $185 and not break again for a year. This concept connects to having a long-term goal alignment between the owner and management company.

Pro tip: replacing high-use fixtures every five to ten years should be accepted practice. Appearance and curb appeal of the property matters greatly to the prospects. If a prospect has ten units to choose from, they will select the one with the most attractive photos online first. If a property does not look good in photos, it will need to be priced 10% to 15% below comparable market units. It's better to rent at market rent and update the units. The net rent collection may be the same, but the ongoing maintenance will be much less in an updated unit.

- Just say "no" to being available 24 hours. Available to whom? Vendors, clients, tenants, or co-workers? It's important to realize the importance of work-life balance and staffing costs. A one-person band can choose to be available 24/7, but it won't take long for them to burn out. The way to achieve long-lasting relationships with proper boundaries is by setting them upfront. If a client is a night owl and can get a hold of you after midnight, they will not be shy about calling again.

If the building has a certain number of units and a history of late-night maintenance tickets, a skeleton night staff may be required.

Every establishment has normal operating hours (for example, 9 a.m. to 5 p.m. Monday to Friday. and Saturday and Sunday 10 a.m. to 4 p.m.). Any time outside normal hours is considered after hours. In a maintenance emergency, there should be a maintenance phone number to call. There is no practical need for staff to be present after hours. Overstaffing can eat away at the collected management fees. Non-profitable management accounts lead to unhappy management companies; they might give up the account, causing the owner to go through the hassle of finding a new management company. No party would be happy in that situation. You can explain to the owner that the operating hours are a measure to keep recurring costs at a reasonable rate and ownership profits high.

If someone's call is missed, just make sure it's returned within a reasonable amount of time. Provide four streams of available communication. Odds are if there is a true emergency, at least one team member will catch it and report the issue. Four streams of communication should include the main portal, email, phone/voice-mail, and text. Another option is hiring a virtual live person to take messages after hours. These services are reasonable and usually involve a fluent English-speaking person who lives overseas.

One exception that should be made for regular after hours contact is when a client lives overseas and wants to have a voice or video chat. Try to set a reasonable time for both parties.

- Just say "no" to remodeling projects inside an occupied unit. Older buildings have the risk of lead-based paint and asbestos. The hassle of moving tenants in and out is greater than the reward of retention or higher rents. The better practice is to vacate the unit, renovate it and find a new tenant. Please follow the local eviction and rent control laws.

The reason so many activities must be refused is a reference back to the 80/20 rule. You must be focused on the activities that produce 80% of the income stream. 20% percent of tenants can cause 80% of the complaints. Drilling down further, 4% can cause 99% of the grievances. Owners' essential needs must be met. However, the additional activities are considered fluff and unnecessary. Do you want to be the king or queen of rent collection and low expenses? Or would you rather be the king or queen of listening to tenant disputes? Which quality will help you earn more money and gain the trust of new clients? If an owner wants to talk nonstop about all the tenant drama they have dealt with over the years, just listen. This is usually the reason that an owner gives up on managing themselves. Owners who allow a personal connection between themselves and the tenants find it difficult to manage the property at arm's length. If you are already managing property, you are familiar with hearing stories of spending 30 hours a week managing one 4-plex building.

Conclusion

For those individuals or groups who are going into the property management industry with the intention to become business owners, knowing the metrics is critical. You should calculate how much fees are expected per unit under management.

For example, let's say each unit generated $1,000 in annual revenue for the company. Overhead for the company can run an average of 30%. After expenses, $700 per unit is left. Remember, the IRS also wants its share of 35%-50% of profits (ask a CPA). After tax, each unit earns the company $455 per year. Each rental market will have a different metric. An apartment renting for $500 per month in an agricultural market versus an apartment renting for $5,000 per month in a metropolitan market will have substantially different metrics to consider. This is just an example.

How many units do you need to have under management for the effort to be worthwhile? How patient do you need to be in building a portfolio before you feel like giving up? Let's reverse engineer the answer. If you want to net $100,000 after taxes, then we divide $100,000 by $450. The answer is 222.22 units. If there are multiple partners, that must also be considered. If two company owners want to net $100,000 after tax, then the company needs to manage 444.44 units.

Let's take a deeper dive.

If the end goal of one is to eventually become an investment property owner, the formula is simple. For example, a duplex costs $800,000. A rental property loan would require at least a 30% down payment for tenant-occupied assets. The cash required for the down payment would be $240,000 plus closing expenses and reserves. For a one-person owner of a company managing 222 units per year, this would require the total net earnings from two years of hard work. ($100,000 year one net income after tax + $100,000 year two net income = $200,000 put towards down payment).

It's important to understand why the building owners are so wealthy and walk the same path! Every business has a finite timeline. There will be a time when you no longer have the energy to stay in the business. The best vehicle to transition to is rental property ownership.

There are scaling issues that should be discussed. How many employees does it take to manage 10, 100, 1,000 units? Can the crew that manages 1,000 units also handle 5,000? If the answer is yes, then the additional units scaled will be pure profit for the business owners. There are sweet spots to stay lean and mean at each portfolio size. It's also easy for expenses to get out of hand. Talented employees will need to be compensated properly.

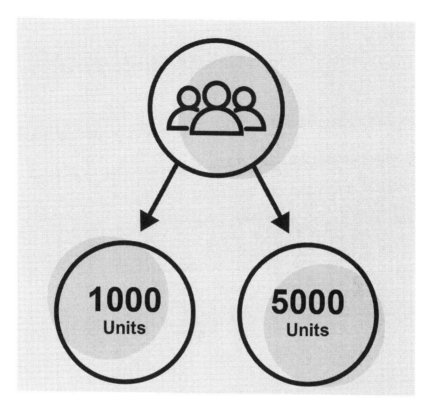

You also need to budget for startup costs. Some of these startup costs are only made once and are not recurring.

The book is almost coming to an end 😟*!* Here are two final tips that will come in handy if implemented.

First Tip: The 80/20 rule. Focus on the most wealth-generating activities first. 20% of the activity spent makes you 80% of your money. These activities would be considered very important goals, such as acquiring the next big property or preparing a property to flip. An activity that is not important in this scenario would be unclogging a toilet or sweeping the laundry room. In real estate management, there are always urgent action items for the maintenance team, but they are not important in the "big picture."

Would you ask your newest team member, fresh out of college (their first job), to select the next apartment complex to purchase? That employee would do their best and could get lucky. However, when there are more experienced team members, it would be best to get their input first. It's ideal when the person or group who is coming up with the funds does the selecting. This concept may seem very simple because it is. The idea is known as "stay in one's lane" (and go for it!). $10/hour payroll should be doing $10/hour tasks. Those who are negotiating $10M-$20M deals may be getting paid $12,000 per hour and should not be distracted with less lucrative tasks.

They say it takes a village to raise a baby. It also takes leverage for business owners to thrive! For all the perfectionists reading this, let go of the 100% perfection scorecard. Once leverage is put in place and everyone stays in their lane, expect the quality control to go down to 90-95% while your wealth doubles, triples, and 10xs. How does that sound?

If everything goes to plan, you might even be able to create leaders within your company so expansion can happen even faster.

Your biggest goal should be the creation of generational wealth for your family. Getting burned out is not an option. When the goal is this juicy, there is no stopping those passionate souls who must accomplish this! Focusing on the main goal will allow your daily, weekly and monthly schedule to align with the ultimate goal for wealth creation. If you're not ready to invest yet, then help create wealth for your clients first. Plant those seeds and get ready to harvest in the spring. When winter comes, you will be ready.

When it comes to delegating management tasks to your own schedule or the team, the 80/20 rule also applies. 80% of the things that keep you up at night (headaches) come from 20% of the tenants. Truthfully, maybe 1% (20% of 20% of 20%) of the tenants cause 99% of the team's headaches. When owner-operators get frustrated, they often generalize, "I can't take it anymore" or "I don't want to deal with the stress." Clients who are too close to the action will often recall their dealings with one tenant from ten years ago. Sound familiar? In reality, if that 1% problem tenant could just be satisfied, they could turn into a raving supporter! Sure, in some cases, relocation is still the desired solution.

Second Tip: Write down your portfolio goal for the next five years. Have your business partners or significant other sign, date it and post it on the wall. *Hold each other accountable.*

Please take some time to write down your goals and share them with someone. (*Fill out the list below*)

My current holdings:

1. Cash Assets:
2. Personal Residence Real Estate:
3. Investment Real Estate:
4. Number of units owned:
5. Number of units managed:

In one year (actual date____) current holdings:

1. Cash Assets:
2. Personal Residence Real Estate:
3. Investment Real Estate:
4. Number of units owned:
5. Number of units managed:

In five years (actual date____) current holdings:

1. Cash Assets:
2. Personal Residence Real Estate:
3. Investment Real Estate:
4. Number of units owned:
5. Number of units managed:

What kind of help do you need to get to reach these goals? Be resourceful; there is always a way to get there. Writing these goals down and posting them on the refrigerator will ingrain them into your psyche and become a part of your new identity. In other words, commit fully 100% to the process!

Epilogue

Congratulations! You made it through the whole book! It's obvious that determination is not an issue for you. Property Management is a lifelong career. Being a great property manager requires having an obsession with procedures and learning. It is easy to be a terrible property manager. To concurrently achieve the goals of owners, tenants, employees and vendors with the utmost professionalism requires years of dedication. Reading this book is a good start or addition to your library of reference materials.

Every day in property management is a day to be surprised and to learn a new lesson. Always carry a notebook so the lesson can be saved and learned from. Read as many books as possible. This book is the condensed version of over 25 years of first-hand experience managing apartments and people. There is always more to learn. The rules of the game seem to change every few months. Technology and politics (landlord-tenant policy) are evolving faster than ever. Documents and disclosures are updated frequently.

Disclaimer: The author holds a Real Estate Broker and General Contractor's license valid in California, USA only. The author does not represent himself as a lawyer, financial planner, or CPA. Each Owner's situation is individual and unique. Everyone should consult with a legal or tax professional for advice that fits one's situation best. The information given in this book comes from a practical perspective. We love all our clients, tenants and fellow landlords. If apartments are operated properly, owners, tenants and landlords are all on one team. This book is written from the viewpoint of the landlord.

Bonus Section

The importance of the physical body. Health is wealth. The most common reason that owners give up the management of their properties is the toll it can take on their physical body, stress and mental health. If you own and manage your own property, you will need strength to pick up a piece of drywall or fix a heavy toilet. If driving around for a couple of hours to see your properties makes your back or hips sore, that should be a wake-up call. Are you having trouble sleeping, or is your family life being adversely affected because you are dealing with these types of issues? Think about what is important in life, then reverse engineer the path.

Super Bonus Section

Once you have achieved financial freedom, please pay the gift forward. If you can partner with a charitable organization or cause, you can help others achieve amazing things while fulfilling your soul simultaneously. Best of luck to all on this windy journey.

I want you to visualize how attainable it is to take $1,000 and turn it into $1M with just a few flips doubling your money. If you don't have $1,000, borrow someone's money and split the profits! Here's why:

$1,000 to $2,000 to $4,000 to $8,000 to $16,000 to $32,000 to $64,000 to $128,000 to $256,000 to $512,000 = $1,026,000!!!!

Photo Album

The following 400+ real-life photos are intended to help you get ready for work in the field. If we were to explain every photo enclosed in this book, it would end up being 700 pages! We go more into detail with the lessons from the photos during our coaching calls.

7 STEP BLUEPRINT TO PASSIVE WEALTH

7 STEP BLUEPRINT TO PASSIVE WEALTH

7 STEP BLUEPRINT TO PASSIVE WEALTH

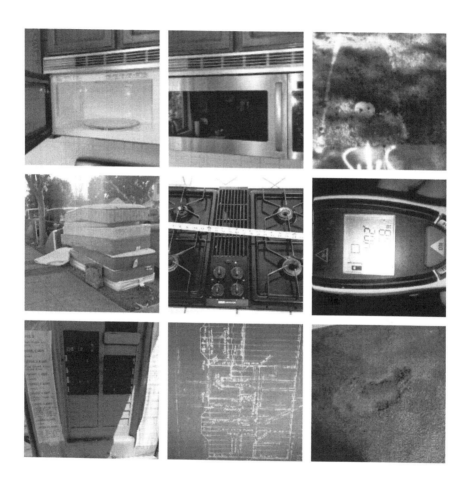

- 211 -

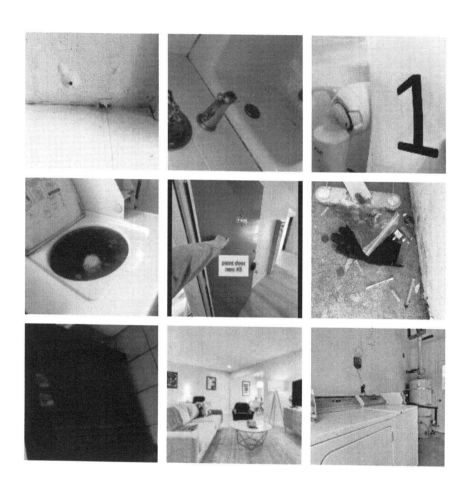

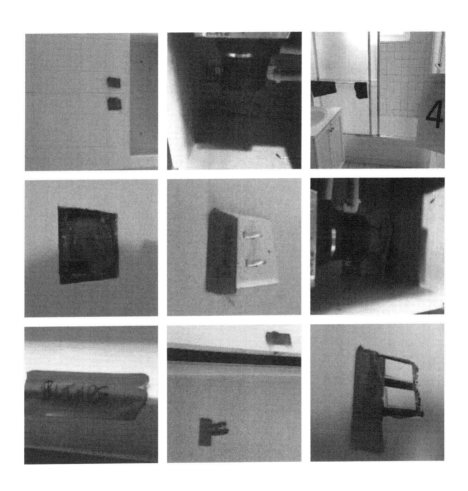

7 STEP BLUEPRINT TO PASSIVE WEALTH

7 STEP BLUEPRINT TO PASSIVE WEALTH

7 STEP BLUEPRINT TO PASSIVE WEALTH

7 STEP BLUEPRINT TO PASSIVE WEALTH

7 STEP BLUEPRINT TO PASSIVE WEALTH

7 STEP BLUEPRINT TO PASSIVE WEALTH

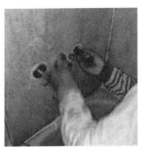

THANK YOU FOR READING MY BOOK!

DOWNLOAD YOUR FREE GIFTS

Just to say thanks for buying and reading my book, I would like to give you a few free bonus gifts, no strings attached!

To Download Now, Visit:
www.RobChiang.com/Freegifts

I appreciate your interest in my book, and I value your feedback as it helps me improve future versions of this book. I would appreciate it if you could leave your invaluable review on Amazon.com with your feedback. Thank you!

References

www.hud.gov

www.census.gov

https://www.census.gov/library/stories/2022/05/housing-vacancy-rates-near-historic-lows.html

https://ipropertymanagement.com/research/renters-vs-homeowners-statistics

https://learn.roofstock.com/blog/rental-property-owner-statistics

https://policyadvice.net/insurance/insights/rental-statistics/

https://www.huduser.gov

www.yardi.com